ISBN 978-0-259-53285-9
PIBN 10822161

1 MONTH OF
FREE
READING

at
www.ForgottenBooks.com

By purchasing this book you are eligible for one month membership to ForgottenBooks.com, giving you unlimited access to our entire collection of over 1,000,000 titles via our web site and mobile apps.

To claim your free month visit:

www.forgottenbooks.com/free822161

English
Français
Deutsche
Italiano
Español
Português

www.forgottenbooks.com

Mythology Photography **Fiction**
Fishing Christianity **Art** Cooking
Essays Buddhism Freemasonry
Medicine **Biology** Music **Ancient
Egypt** Evolution Carpentry Physics
Dance Geology **Mathematics** Fitness
Shakespeare **Folklore** Yoga Marketing
Confidence Immortality Biographies
Poetry **Psychology** Witchcraft
Electronics Chemistry History **Law**
Accounting **Philosophy** Anthropology
Alchemy Drama Quantum Mechanics
Atheism Sexual Health **Ancient History**
Entrepreneurship Languages Sport
Paleontology Needlework Islam
Metaphysics Investment Archaeology
Parenting Statistics Criminology
Motivational

Jan. 1911 . [illegible]

6613
48

[illegible]

See - Publications of the Colonial Society of Mass. vol. 11 (1906-7) p. 15-?

Lo, Allen, *copied from British*
His twitches broke by biting nails,
Appears in Hyperborean skies
To tell the world the Bible lies

. . . .

Behold him more, ye staunch divines!
His tall head bristling thro' the pines;
All front he reems into wall of brass
And brays tremendous as an Ass;
One hand is clenched to batter noses
While t'other scrawls 'gainst Paul
and Moses.

Samuel Hopkins Quot. in
Mitchell's American Lands and
Letters vol. p. 163.

"He named his book the Oracles of Reason
after a wretched publication of Charles Blount
··· probably Allen's favorite author, and not
improbably the only one whose works he had
read. This was the first formal publication in the U.S. openly directed against
the Christian Religion"
T. Dwight, Travels ch. 2 p. 407

"The book was equally bad in argument and style. It was wickedly ridiculed, very little read, and is now wholly forgotten."

—Eliot: Biog. Dict. p. 25

REASON,

THE

ONLY ORACLE OF MAN;

OR A COMPENDIOUS

SYSTEM OF NATURAL RELIGION.

BY COL. ETHAN ALLEN.

BOSTON:

J. P. MENDUM, CORNHILL.

1854.

102
Allen

(Fenn)

INTRODUCTION.

COLONEL ETHAN ALLEN, the author of Oracles of Reason, was the son of Joseph Allen, a native of Coventry, Connecticut, a farmer in moderate circumstances. He afterwards resided in Litchfield, where Ethan was born in the year 1739. The family consisted of eight children, of whom our author was the eldest. But few incidents connected with his early life are known. We are apprised, however, that notwithstanding his education was very limited, his ambition to prove himself worthy of that attention which superior intellect ever commands, induced him diligently to explore every subject that came under his notice. A stranger to fear, his opinions were ever given without disguise or hesitation; and an enemy to oppression, he sought every opportunity to redress the wrongs of the oppressed.

At the breaking out of the Revolutionary War, he raised in Vermont, where he had resided, a company of volunteers, consisting of two hundred and thirty, with which he surprised the fortress of Ticonderoga, May 10, 1775, containing about forty men, and one hundred pieces of cannon. He was unfortunately taken prisoner in September following, in an attempt on Montreal, and suffered a cruel imprisonment for several years. For an account of which, the reader is referred to his narrative, contained in a memoir of the author, by Mr. Hugh Moore, Plattsburg, 1834.

Soon after the close of the revolution, Col. Allen composed the following work; which, on account of the bold and unusual manner, particularly in this country, that the subject of religion is treated, he had great difficulty to get published. It lay a long time in the hands of a printer at Hartford, who had not the moral courage to print it.

It was finally printed by a Mr. Haswell, of Bennington, Vt. in 1784. Not long after its publication, a part of the edition, comprising the entire of several signatures, was accidentally consumed by fire. Whether Mr. H. deemed this fire a judgment upon him for having printed the work or not, is unknown—but, the fact is, he soon after committed the remainder of the edition to the flames, and joined the Methodist Connection; so that but few copies were circulated.

COL. ALLEN died in the town of Burlington, Vt., on the 12th of February, 1789, of apoplexy.

PREFACE.

An apology appears to me to be impertinent in writers who venture their works to public inspection, for this obvious reason, that if they need it, they should have been stifled in the birth, and not permitted a public existence. I therefore offer my composition to the candid judgment of the impartial world without it, taking it for granted that I have as good a natural right to expose myself to public censure, by endeavouring to subserve mankind, as any of the species who have published their productions since the creation; and I ask no favor at the hands of philosophers, divines or critics, but hope and expect they will severely chastise me for my errors and mistakes, least they may have a share in perverting the truth, which is very far from my intention.

In the circle of my acquaintance, (which has not been small,) I have generally been denominated a Deist, the reality of which I never disputed, being conscious I am no Christian, except mere infant baptism make me one; and as to being a Deist, I know not, strictly speaking, whether I am one or not, for I have never read their writings; mine will therefore determine the matter; for I have not in the least disguised my sentiments, but have written freely without any conscious knowledge of prejudice for, or against any man, sectary or party whatever; but wish that good sense, truth and virtue may be promoted and flourish in the world, to the detection of delusion, superstition, and false religion; and therefore my errors in the succeeding treatise, which may be rationally pointed out, will be readily rescinded.

By the public's most obedient and humble servant.

ETHAN ALLEN.

ORACLES OF REASON.

CHAPTER I.

SECTION I.

THE DUTY OF REFORMING MANKIND FROM SUPERSTITION AND ERROR, AND THE GOOD CONSEQUENCES OF IT.

THE desire of knowledge has engaged the attention of the wise and curious among mankind in all ages which has been productive of extending the arts and sciences far and wide in the several quarters of the globe, and excited the contemplative to explore nature's laws in a gradual series of improvement, until philosophy, astronomy, geography, and history, with many other branches of science, have arrived to a great degree of perfection.

It is nevertheless to be regretted, that the bulk of mankind, even in those nations which are most celebrated for learning and wisdom, are still carried down the torrent of superstition, and entertain very unworthy apprehensions of the BEING, PERFECTIONS, CREATION, and PROVIDENCE of GOD, and their duty to him, which lays an indispensable obligation on the philosophic friends of human nature, unanimously to exert themselves in every lawful, wise, and prudent method, to

endeavor to reclaim mankind from their ignorance
and delusion, by enlightening their minds in those
great and sublime truths concerning God and his
providence, and their obligations to moral rectitude,
which in this world, and that which is to come, cannot fail greatly to affect their happiness and well
being.

Though "none by searching can find out God, or
the Almighty to perfection," yet I am persuaded, that
if mankind would dare to exercise their reason as
freely on those divine topics as they do in the common
concerns of life, they would, in a great measure, rid
themselves of their blindness and superstition, gain
more exalted ideas of God and their obligations to
him and one another, and be proportionally delighted
and blessed with the views of his moral government,
make better members of society, and acquire many
powerful incentives to the practice of morality, which
is the last and greatest perfection that human nature
is capable of.

SECTION II.

OF THE BEING OF A GOD.

THE laws of nature having subjected mankind to a
state of absolute dependence on something out of it,
and manifestly beyond themselves, or the compound
exertion of their natural powers, gave them the first
conception of a superior principle existing; otherwise
they could have had no possible conception of a superintending power. But this sense of dependency,
which results from experience and reasoning on the
facts, which every day cannot fail to produce, has

uniformly established the knowledge of our dependence to every individual of the species who are rational, which necessarily involves, or contains in it,
the idea of a ruling power, or that there is a God,
which ideas are synonymous.

The globe with its productions, the planets in their
motions, and the starry heavens in their magnitudes,
surprise our senses and confound our reason, in their
munificent lessons of instruction concerning God, by
means whereof, we are apt to be more or less lost in
our ideas of the object of divine adoration, though at
the same time every one is truly sensible that their
being and preservation is from God. We are too apt
to confound our ideas of God with his works, and
take the latter for the former. Thus barbarous and
unlearned nations have imagined, that inasmuch as
the sun in its influence is beneficial to them in bringing forward the spring of the year, causing the production of vegetation, and food for their subsistence,
that therefore it is their God: while others have lo-
cated other parts of creation, and ascribe to them
prerogatives of God; and mere creatures and images
have been substituted for Gods by the wickedness or
weakness of man, or both together. It seems that
mankind in most ages and parts of the world have
been fond of corporeal Deities with whom their out-
ward senses might be gratified, or as fantastically di-
verted from the just apprehension of the true God, by
a supposed supernatural intercourse with invisible and
mere spiritual beings, to whom they ascribe divinity,
so that through one means or other, the character of
the true God has been much neglected, to the great
detriment of truth, justice, and morality in the world;
nor is it possible that mankind can be uniform in their

religious opinions, or worship God according to knowledge, except they can form a consistent arrangement
of ideas of the Divine character.

Although we extend our ideas retrospectively ever
so far upon the succession, yet no one cause in the
extended order of succession, which depends upon
another prior to itself, can be the independent cause
of all things : nor is it possible to trace the order of
the succession of causes back to that self-existent
cause, inasmuch as it is eternal and infinite, and cannot therefore be traced out by succession, which operates according to the order of time, consequently
can bear no more proportion to the eternity of God,
than time itself may be supposed to do, which has no
proportion at all; as the succeeding arguments respecting the eternity and infinity of God will evince.
But notwithstanding the series of the succession of
causes cannot be followed in a retrospective succession
up to the self-existent or eternal cause, it is nevertheless a perpetual and conclusive evidence of a God.—
For a succession of causes considered collectively, can
be nothing more than effects of the independent cause,
and as much dependent on it as those dependent
causes are upon one another; so that we may with
certainty conclude that the system of nature, which
we call by the name of natural causes, is as much
dependent on a self-existent cause, as an individual of
the species in the order of generation is dependent on
its progenitors for existence.   Such part of the series
of nature's operations, which we understand, has a
regular and necessary connection with, and dependence on its parts, which we denominate by the names
of cause and effect.   From hence we are authorised
from reason to conclude, that the vast system of

causes and effects are thus necessarily connected, (speaking of the natural world only,) and the whole regularly and necessarily dependent on a self-existent cause; so that we are obliged to admit an independent cause, and ascribe self-existence to it, otherwise it could not be independent, and consequently not a God. But the eternity or manner of the existence of a self-existent and independent being is to all finite capacities utterly incomprehensible; yet this is so far from an objection against the reality of such a being, that it is essentially necessary to support the evidence of it; for if we could comprehend that being whom we call God, he would not be God, but must have been finite and that in the same degree as those may be supposed to be who could comprehend him; therefore so certain that God is, we cannot comprehend his essence, eternity, or manner of existence. This should always be premised, when we assay to reason on the being, perfection, eternity, and infinity of God, or of his creation and providence. As far as we understand nature, we are become acquainted with the character of God, for the knowledge of nature is the revelation of God. If we form in our imagination a compendious idea of the harmony of the universe, it is the same as calling God by the name of harmony, for there could be no harmony without regulation, and no regulation without a regulator, which is expressive of the idea of a God. Nor could it be possible, that there could be order or disorder, except we admit of such a thing as creation, and creation contains in it the idea of a creator, which is another appellation for the Divine Being, distinguishing God from his creation. Furthermore, there could be no proportion, figure, or motion, without wisdom and power; wisdom to plan, and power to execute, and these are perfections, when applied to the works of nature, which signify the agency or superintendency of God. If we consider nature to be matter, figure, and motion, we include the idea of God in that of motion ; for motion implies a mover as much as creation does a creator.   If from the composition, texture, and tendency of the universe in general, we form a complex idea of general good resulting therefrom to mankind, we implicitly admit a God by the name of good, including the idea of his providence to man.   And from hence arises our obligations to love and adore God, because he provides for, and is beneficent to us.   Abstract the idea of goodness from the character of God, and it would cancel all our obligations to him, and excite us to hate and detest him as a tyrant : hence it is, that ignorant people are superstitiously misled into a conceit that they hate God, when at the same time it is only the idol of their own imagination, which they truly ought to hate and be ashamed of ; but were such persons to connect the ideas of power, wisdom, goodness, and all possible perfection in the character of God, their hatred towards him would be turned into love and adoration.

By extending our ideas in a larger circle, we shall perceive our dependence on the earth and waters of the globe which we inhabit, and from which we are bountifully fed and gorgeously arrayed ; and next extend our ideas to the sun, whose fiery mass darts its brilliant rays of light to our terraqueous ball with amazing velocity, and whose region of inexhaustible fire supplies it with fervent heat, which causes vegetation, and gilds the various seasons of the year with ten thousand charms : this is not the achievement of

-man, but the workmanship and providence of God. But how the sun is supplied with materials, thus to perpetuate its kind influences, we know not. But will any one deny the reality of those beneficial influences, because we do not understand the manner of the perpetuality of that fiery world, or how it became such a body of fire? or will any one deny the reality of nutrition by food, because we do not understand the secret operation of the digesting powers of animal nature, or the minute particulars of its cherishing influence? None will be so stupid as to do it. Equally absurd would it be for us to deny the providence of God, by "whom we live, move, and have our being," because we cannot comprehend it.

We know that earth, water, fire and air, in their various compositions subserve us, and we also know that these elements are devoid of reflection, reason, or design; from whence we may easily infer, that a wise, understanding, and designing being has ordained them to be thus subservient. Could blind chance constitute order and decorum, and consequently a providence? That wisdom, order, and design should be the production of nonentity, or of chaos, confusion, and old night, is too absurd to deserve a serious confutation, for it supposeth that there may be effects without a cause, viz.: produced by nonentity, or that chaos and confusion could produce the effects of power, wisdom, and goodness. Such absurdities as these we must assent to, or subscribe to the doctrine of a self-existent and providential being.

SECTION III.

THE MANNER OF DISCOVERING THE MORAL PERFECTIONS AND AT-
TRIBUTES OF GOD.

HAVING in a concise manner offered a variety of in-
disputable reasons to evince the certainty of the being
and providence of God, and of his goodness to man
through the intervention of the series of nature's operations, which are commonly described by the name
of natural causes, we come now more particularly to
the consideration of his moral perfections; and though
all finite beings fall as much short of an adequate
knowledge thereof as they do of perfection itself, nevertheless through the intelligence of our own souls we
may have something of a prospective idea of the divine perfections.   For though the human mind bears
no proportion to the divine, yet there is undoubtedly
a resemblance between them.   For instance, God
knows all things, and we know some things, and in
the things which we do understand, our knowledge
agrees with that of the divine, and cannot fail necessarily corresponding with it.   To more than know a
thing, speaking of that thing only, is impossible even
to omniscience itself; for knowledge is but the same
in both the infinite and finite minds.   To know a
thing is the same as to have right ideas of it, or ideas
according to truth, and truth is uniform in all rational
minds, the divine mind not excepted.   It will not be
disputed but that mankind in plain and common
matters understand justice from injustice, truth from
falsehood, right from wrong, virtue from vice, and
praise-worthiness from blame-worthiness, for other

wise they could not be accountable creatures. This being admitted, we are capable of forming a complex idea of a moral character, which when done in the most deliberate, the wisest, and most rational manner in our power, we are certain bears a resemblance to the divine perfections. For as we learn from the works of nature an idea of the power and wisdom of God, so from our own rational nature we learn an idea of his moral perfections.

From what has been observed on the moral perfections of God, we infer that all rational beings, who have an idea of justice, goodness, and truth, have at the same time either a greater or less idea of the moral perfections of God. It is by reason that we are able to compound an idea of a moral character, whether applied to God or man; it is that which gives us the supremacy over the irrational part of the creation.

SECTION IV.

THE CAUSE OF IDOLATRY, AND THE REMEDY OF IT.

INASMUCH as God is not corporeal, and consequently does not and cannot come within the notice of our bodily sensations, we are therefore obliged to deduce inferences from his providence, and particularly from our own rational nature, in order to form our conceptions of the divine character, which through inattention, want of learning, or through the natural imbecility of mankind, or through the artifice of designing men, or all together, they have been greatly divided and subdivided in their notions of a God. Many have so groped in the dark as wholly to mistake the proper

1 *

object of divine worship, and not distinguishing the
creator from his creation, have paid adoration to "four
footed beasts and creeping things." And some have
ascribed divine honors to the sun, moon, or stars;
while others have been infatuated to worship dumb,
senseless, and unintelligent idols, which derived their
existence as Gods, partly from mechanics, who gave
them their figure, proportion, and beauty, and partly
from their priests, who gave them their attributes;
whose believers, it appears, were so wrought upon,
that they cried out in the ecstasy of their deluded zeal,
"Great is Diana." Whatever delusions have taken
place in the world relative to the object of divine worship, or respecting the indecencies or immoralities of
the respective superstitions themselves, or by what
means soever introduced or perpetuated, whether by
designing men whose interest it has always been to
impose on the weakness of the great mass of the vulgar; or as it is probable, that part of those delusions
took place in consequence of the weakness of unculti-
vated reason, in deducing a visible instead of an invisible God from the works of nature. Be that as it
will, mankind are generally possessed of an idea that
there is a God, however they may have been mistaken
or misled as to the object. This notion of a God, as
has been before observed, must have originated from
a universal sense of dependence, which mankind have
on something that is more wise, powerful, and beneficent than themselves, or they could have had no apprehensions of any superintending principle in the
universe, and consequently would never have sought
after a God, or have had any conception of his existence, nor could designing men . have imposed on their
credulity by obtruding false Gods upon them; but

taking advantage of the common belief that there is a
God, they artfully deceive their adherents with regard
to the object to be adored. There are other sorts of
idols which have no existence but in the mere imagination of the human mind; and these are vastly the
most numerous, and universally (either in the greater
or less degree) dispersed over the world; the wisest
of mankind are not and cannot be wholly exempt
from them, inasmuch as every wrong conception of
God is (as far as the error takes place in the mind)
idolatrous. To give a sample, an idea of a jealous
God is of this sort. Jealousy is the offspring of finite ·
minds, proceeding from the want of knowledge, which
· in dubious matters makes us suspicious and distrustful; but in matters which we clearly understand,
there can be no jealousy, for knowledge excludes it,
so that to ascribe it to God is a manifest infringement
on his omniscience.*

The idea of a revengeful God is likewise one of ·
that sort, but this idea of divinity being borrowed
from a savage nature, needs no further confutation.
The representation of a God, who (as we are told by
certain divines) from all eternity elected an inconsiderable part of mankind to eternal life, and reprobated
the rest to eternal damnation, merely from his own
sovereignty, adds another to the number;—this representation of the Deity undoubtedly took its rise from
that which we discovered in great, powerful, and
wicked tyrants among men, however tradition may
since have contributed to its support, though I am ap-
prehensive that a belief in those who adhere to that
doctrine, that they themselves constitute that blessed

* "The Lord thy God is a jealous God."

elect number, has been a greater inducement to them to close with it, than all other motives added together. It is a selfish and inferior notion of a God void of justice, goodness, and truth, and has a natural tendency to impede the cause of true religion and morality in the world, and diametrically repugnant to the truth of the divine character, and which, if admitted to be true, overturns all religion, wholly precluding the agency of mankind in either their salvation or damnation, resolving the whole into the sovereign disposal of a tyrannical and unjust being, which is offensive to reason and common sense, and subversive of moral rectitude in general. But as it was not my design so much to confute the multiplicity of false representations of a God, as to represent just and consistent ideas of the true God, I shall therefore omit any further observation on them in this place, with this remark, that all unjust representations, or ideas of God, are so. many detractions from his character among mankind. To remedy these idolatrous notions of a God, it is requisite to form right and consistent ideas in their stead.

The discovery of truth necessarily excludes error from the mind, which nothing else can possibly do; for some sort of God or other will crowd itself into the conceptions of dependent creatures, and if they are not so happy as to form just ones, they will substitute erroneous and delusive ones in their stead; so that it serves no valuable purpose to mankind, to confute their idolatrous opinions concerning God, without communicating to them just notions concerning the true one, for if this is not effected, nothing is done to the purpose. For, as has been before observed, mankind will form to themselves, or receive from others, an idea of Divinity either right or wrong : this is the universal voice of intelligent nature, from whence a weighty and conclusive argument may be drawn of the reality of a God, however inconsistent most of their conceptions of him may be. The fact is, mankind readily perceives that there is a God, by feeling their dependence on him, and as they explore his works, and observe his providence, which is too sublime for finite capacities to understand but in part, they have been more or less confounded in their discoveries of a just idea of a God and of his moral government. Therefore we should exercise great applications and care whenever we assay to speculate upon the Divine character, accompanied with a sincere desire after truth, and not ascribe anything to his perfections or government which is inconsistent with reason or the best information which we are able to apprehend of moral rectitude, and be at least wise enough not to charge God with injustice and contradictions which we should scorn to be charged with ourselves. No king, governor, or parent would like to be accused of partiality in their respective governments, " Is it fit to say unto Princes, ye are ungodly, how much less to him that regardeth not the persons of princes, or the rich more than the poor, for they are all the work of his hands."

2

CHAPTER II.

SECTION I.

OF THE ETERNITY OF CREATION.

As creation was the result of eternal and infinite wisdom, justice, goodness, and truth, and effected by infinite power, it is like its great author, mysterious to us. How it could be accomplished, or in what manner performed, can never be comprehended by any capacity.

Eternal, whether applied to duration, existence, action, or creation, is incomprehensible to us, but implies no contradiction in either of them; for that which is above comprehension we cannot perceive to be contradictory, nor on the other hand can we perceive its rationality or consistency. We are certain that God is a rational, wise, understanding Being, because he has in degree made us so, and his wisdom, power, and goodness is visible to us in his creation, and government of the world. From these facts we are rationally induced to acknowledge him, and not because we can comprehend his being, perfections, creation, or providence. Could we comprehend God, he would cease to be what he is. The ignorant among men cannot comprehend the understanding of the wise among their own species, much less the perfection of a God; nevertheless, in our ratiocination upon the works and harmony of nature, we are obliged to concede to a self-existent and eternal cause of all things, as has been sufficiently argued, though at the same time it is mysterious to us, that there should be such a being as a self-existent and eternally independent one;—thus we believe in God, although we cannot comprehend anything of the how, why or wherefore it was possible for him to be; and as creation was the exertion of such an incomprehensible and perfect being, it must of necessary consequence be, in a great measure, mysterious to us. We can nevertheless be certain, that it has been of an equal eternity and infinitude of extension with God.

Immensity being replete with creation, the omniscient, omnipresent, omnipotent, eternal, and infinite exertion of God in creation, is incomprehensible to the understanding or the weakness of man, and will eternally remain the prerogative of infinite penetration, sagacity, and uncreated intelligence to understand.

SECTION II.

OBSERVATIONS OF MOSES'S ACCOUNT OF CREATION.

THE foregoing theory of creation and providence will probably be rejected by most people in this country, inasmuch as they are prepossessed with the theology of Moses, which represents creation to have a beginning. " In the beginning God created the heavens and the earth." In the preceding part of this chapter it has been evinced that creation and providence could not have had a beginning, and that they are not circumscribed, but unlimited; yet it seems that Moses limited creation by a prospective view of the heavens, or firmament from this globe, and if creation was thus limited, it would consequently have circumscribed the dominion and display of the divine providence or perfection; but if Moses's idea of the creation of "the heavens and the earth," was immense, ever so many days of progressive work could never have finished such a boundless creation; for a progressive creation is the same as a limited one; as each progressive day's work would be bounded by a successive admeasurement, and the whole six days' work added together could be but local, and bear no manner of proportion to infinitude, but would limit the dominion, and consequently the display of the divine perfections or providence, which is incompatible with a just idea of eternity and infinity of God, as has been argued in the foregoing pages.

There are a variety of other blunders in Moses's description of creation, one of which I shall mention, which is to be found in his history of the first and fourth day's work of God: "And God said, Let there be light, and there was light; and God called the light day, and the darkness he called night: and the evening and the morning were the first day." Then he proceeds to the second and third day's work, and so on to the sixth; but in his chronicle of the fourth day's work, he says that "God made two great lights, the greater light to rule the day, and the lesser light to rule the night." This appears to be an inconsistent history of the origin of light. Day and night were ordained the first day, and on the fourth day the greater and less lights were made to serve the same purposes; but it is likely that many errors have crept into his writings, through the vicissitudes of learning, and particularly from the corruptions of translations, of his as well as the writings of other ancient authors; besides, it must be acknowledged that those ancient writers labored under great difficulties in writ-

ing to posterity, merely from the consideration of the
infant state of learning and knowledge then in the
world, and consequently we should not act the part of
severe critics, with their writings, any further than to
prevent their obtrusion on the world as being infallible.

SECTION III.

OF THE ETERNITY AND INFINITUDE OF DIVINE PROVIDENCE.

WHEN we consider our solar system, attracted by
its fiery centre, and moving in its several orbits, with
regular, majestic, and periodical revolutions, we are
charmed at the prospect and contemplation of those
worlds of motions, and adore the wisdom and power
by which they are attracted, and their velocity regulated and perpetuated. And when we reflect that the
blessings of life are derived from, and dependent on,
the properties, qualities, constructions, proportions and
movements, of that stupendous machine, we grate-
fully acknowledge the divine beneficence. When we
extend our thoughts (through our external sensations)
to the vast regions of the starry heavens, we are lost
in the immensity of God's works. Some stars appear fair and luminous, and others scarcely discerni-
ble to the eye, which by the help of glasses make a
brilliant appearance, bringing the knowledge of others
far remote, within the verge of our feeble discoveries,
which merely by the eye could not have been discerned or distinguished. These discoveries of the
works of God naturally prompt the inquisitive mind
to conclude that the author of this astonishing part of
creation which is displayed to our view, has still ex-

tended his creation; so that if it were possible that any of us could be transported to the farthest extended star, which is perceptible to us here, we should from thence survey worlds as distant from that as that is from this, and so on *ad infinitum.*

Furthermore, it is altogether reasonable to conclude that the heavenly bodies, *alias* worlds, which move or are situate within the circle of our knowledge, as well all others throughout immensity, are each and every one of them possessed or inhabited by some intelligent agents or other, however different their sensations or manners of receiving or communicating their ideas may be from ours, or however different from each other. For why would it not have been as wise or as consistent with the perfections which we adore in God, to have neglected giving being to intelligence in this world as in those other worlds, interspersed with æther of various qualities in his immense creation? And inasmuch as this world is thus replenished, we may, with the highest rational certainty infer, that as God has given us to rejoice, and adore him for our being, he has acted consistent with his goodness, in the display of his providence throughout the university of worlds.

To suppose that God Almighty has confined his goodness to this world, to the exclusion of all others, is much similar to the idle fancies of some individuals in this world, that they, and those of their communion or faith, are the favorites of heaven exclusively; but these are narrow and bigotted conceptions, which are degrading to a rational nature, and utterly unworthy of God, of whom we should form the most exalted ideas.

It may be objected that a man cannot subsist in the

sun; but does it follow from thence, that God cannot
or has not constituted a nature peculiar to that fiery
region, and caused it to be as natural and necessary
for it to suck in and breathe out flames of fire, as it
is for us to do the like in air. Numerous are the
kinds of fishy animals which can no other way subsist but in the water, in which other animals would
perish, (amphibious ones excepted,) while other animals, in a variety of forms, either swifter or slower
move on the surface of the earth, or wing the air. Of
these there are sundry kinds, which during the season
of winter live without food ; and many of the insects
which are really possessed of animal life, remain fro-
zen, and as soon as they are let loose by the kind influence of the sun, they again assume their wonted
animal life ; and if animal life may differ so much in
the same world, what inconceivable variety may be
possible in worlds innumerable, as applicable to mental, cogitative, and organized beings. Certain it is,
that any supposed obstructions, concerning the quality
or temperature of any or every one of those worlds,
could not have been any bar in the way of God Almighty, with regard to his replenishing his universal
creation with moral agents. The unlimited perfection
of God could perfectly well adapt every part of his
creation to the design of whatever rank or species of
constituted beings, his Godlike wisdom and goodness
saw fit to impart existence to ; so that as there is no
deficiency of absolute perfection in God, it is rationally demonstrative that the immense creation is replenished with rational agents, and that it has been
eternally so, and that the display of divine goodness
must have been as perfect and complete, in the ante-
cedent, as it is possible to be in the subsequent eternity.

From this theological way of arguing on the creation and providence of God, it appears that the whole, which we denominate by the term *nature*, which is the same as creation perfectly regulated, was eternally connected together by the creator to answer the same all glorious purpose, *to wit :* the display of the divine nature, the consequences of which are existence and happiness to beings in general, so that creation, with all its productions operates according to the laws of nature, and is sustained by the self-existent eternal cause, in perfect order and decorum, agreeable to the eternal wisdom, unalterable rectitude, impartial justice, and immense goodness of the divine nature, which is a summary of God's providence. It is from the established order of nature. that summer and winter, rainy and fair seasons, moonshine, refreshing breezes, seed time and harvest, day and night, interchangeably succeed each other, and diffuse their extensive blessings to man. Every enjoyment and support of life is from God, delivered to his creatures in and by the tendency, aptitude, disposition, and operation of those laws. Nature is the medium, or intermediate instrument through which God dispenses his benignity to mankind. The air we breathe in, the light of the sun, and the waters of the murmuring rills, evince his providence : and well it is, that they are given in so great profusion, that they cannot by the monopoly of the rich be engrossed from the poor.

When we copiously pursue the study of nature, we are certain to be lost in the immensity of the works and wisdom of God; we may nevertheless, in a variety of things discern their fitness, happifying tendency and sustaining quality to us ward, from all which, as rational and contemplative beings we are prompted to infer, that God is universally uniform and consistent in his infinitude of creation and providence, although we cannot comprehend all that consistency, by reason of infirmity ; yet we are morally sure, of all possible plans, infinite wisdom must have eternally adopted the best, and infinite goodness have approved it, and infinite power have perfected it. And as the good of beings in general must have been the ultimate end of God in his creation and government of his creatures, his omniscience could not fail to have it always present in his view. Universal nature must therefore be ultimately attracted to this single point, and infinite perfection must have eternally displayed itself in creation and providence. From hence we infer, that God is as eternal and infinite in his goodness, as his self-existent and perfect nature is omnipotently great.

SECTION IV.

THE PROVIDENDE OF GOD DOES NOT INTERFERE WITH THE AGENCY OF MAN.

THE doctrine of Fate has been made use of in armies as a policy to induce soldiers to face danger. Mahomet taught his army that the " term of every man's life was fixed by God, and that none could shorten it, by any hazard that he might seem to be exposed to in battle or otherwise," but that it should be introduced into peaceable and civil life, and be patronized by any teachers of religion, is quite strange, as it subverts religion in general, and renders the teaching of it unnecessary, except among other necessary events it may be premised that it is necessary they teach that doctrine, and that I oppose it from the influence of the same law of fate upon which thesis we are all disputing and acting in certain necessary circles, and if so, I make another necessary movement, which is, to discharge the public teachers of this doctrine, and expend their salaries in an economical manner, which might better answer the purposes of our happiness, or lay it out in good wine or old spirits to make the heart glad, and laugh at the stupidity or cunning of those who would have made us mere machines.

Some advocates for the doctrine of fate will also maintain that we are free agents, notwithstanding they tell us there has been a concatination of causes and events which has reached from God down to this time, and which will eternally be continued — that has and will control, and bring about every action of our lives, though there is not anything in nature more certain than that we cannot act necessarily and freely in the same action, and at the same time; yet it is hard for such persons, who have verily believed that they are elected, (and thus by a predetermination of God become his special favorites,) to give up their notions of a predetermination of all events, upon which system their election and everlasting happiness is nonsensically founded; and on the other hand, it is also hard for them to go so evidently against the law of naturn (or dictates of conscience) which intuitively evinces the certainty of human liberty, as to reject such evidence; and therefore hold to both parts of the contradiction, *to wit*, that they act necessarily, and freely, upon which contradictory principle they endeavored to maintain the dictates of natural conscience, and also their darling. folly of being electedly and exclusively favorites of God.

CHAPTER III.

SECTION I.

THE DOCTRINE OF THE INFINITY OF EVIL AND OF SIN CONSIDERED.

THAT God is infinitely good in the eternal displays of his providence, has been argued in the third section of the second chapter, from which we infer that there cannot be an infinite evil in the universe, inasmuch as it would be incompatible with infinite good; yet there are many who imbibe the doctrine of the infinite evil of sin, and the maxim on which they predicate their arguments in its support, are, that the greatness of sin, or adequateness of its punishment, is not to be measured, or its viciousness ascertained by the capacity and circumstances of the offender, but by the capacity and dignity of the being against whom the offence is committed; and as every transgression is against the authority and law of God, it is therefore against God; and as God is infinite, therefore, sin is an infinite evil, and from hence infer the infinite and vindictive wrath of God against sinners, and of his justice in dooming them, as some say to infinite, and others say to eternal misery: the one without degree or measure, and the other without end or duration.

Admitting this maxim for truth, that the transgressions or sins of mankind are to be estimated by their heinousness, by the dignity and infinity of the divine nature, then it will follow that all sins would be equal, which would confound all our notions of the degrees or aggravations of sin; so that the sin would be the same to kill my neighbor as it would be to kill his

horse. For the divine nature, by this maxim, being
the rule by which man's sin is to be estimated, and
always the same, there could therefore be no degrees
in sin or guilt, any more than there are degrees of
perfection in God, whom we all admit to be infinite,
and who for that reason only cannot admit of any degrees or enlargement. Therefore as certain as there
are degrees in sin, the infinity of the divine nature
cannot be the standard whereby it is to be ascertained,
which single consideration is a sufficient confutation
of the doctrine of the infinite evil of sin, as predicated
on that maxim, inasmuch as none are so stupid as not
to discern that there are degrees and aggravations in
sin.

I recollect a discourse of a learned Ecclesiastic, who
was laboring in support of this doctrine. His first
proposition was, "That moral rectitude was infinitely
pleasing to God;" from which he deduced this inference, viz., "That a contrariety to moral rectitude
was consequently infinitely displeasing to God and
infinitely evil." That the absolute moral rectitude of
the divine nature is infinitely well pleasing to God,
will not be disputed; for this is none other but perfect
and infinite rectitude; but there cannot in nature be
an infinite contrariety thereto, or any being infinitely
evil, or infinite in any respect whatever, except we
admit a self-existent and infinite diabolical nature,
which is too absurd to deserve argumentative confutation. Therefore, as all possible moral evil must result from the agency of finite beings, consisting in
their sinful deviations from the rules of eternal unerring order and reason, which is moral rectitude in the
abstract, we infer that, provided *all finite beings in
the universe* had not done anything else but sin and

rebel against God, reason and moral rectitude in general; all possible moral evil would fall as much short of being infinite, as all finite capacities, complexly considered, would fail of being infinite, which will bear no proportion at all. For though *finite minds*, as has been before argued, bear a *resemblance to God*, yet they bear *no proportion* to his *infinity*; and therefore there is not and cannot be any being, beings or agency of being or beings, complexly considered or otherwise, which are infinite in capacity, or which are infinitely evil and detestable in the sight of God, in that unlimited sense; for the *actions* or *agency* of *limited beings*, are also *limited*, which is the same as *finite:* so that both the virtues and vices of man are finite; they are not virtuous or vicious but in degree; therefore moral evil is finite and bounded.

Though there is one, and but one infinite good, which is God, and there can be no dispute, but that God judges, and approves or disapproves of all things and beings, and agencies of beings, as in truth they are, or in other words judges of every thing as being what it is; but to judge a *finite evil* to be *infinite*, would be *infinitely erroneous* and disproportionable; for so certain as there is a distinction between *infinity* and *infinitude*, so certain finite *sinful agency* cannot be infinitely evil; or in other words *finite offences* cannot be *infinite.* Nor is it possible that the greatest of sinners should in justice deserve infinite punishment, or their nature sustain it; *finite beings* may as well be supposed to be capable of *infinite happiness* as of *infinite misery*, but the rank which they hold in the universe exempts them from either; it nev-

2

ertheless admits them to a state of agency, probation or
trial, consequently to interchangeable progressions in
moral good and evil, and of course to alternate happiness or misery. We will dismiss the doctrine of the
infinite evil of sin with this observation, that as no *mere
creature* can suffer an *infinitude* of misery or of punishment, it is therefore incompatible with the wisdom of
God, so far to capacitate creatures to sin, as in his constitution of things to foreclose himself from *adequately*
punishing them for it.

SECTION II.

THE MORAL GOVERNMENT OF GOD AS INCOMPATIBLE WITH ETERNAL PUNISHMENT.

WE may for certain conclude, that such a punishment will never have the divine approbation, or be
inflicted on any intelligent being or beings in the infinitude of the government of God. For an endless punishment defeats the very end of its institution, which in
all wise and good governments is as well to reclaim
offenders, as to be examples to others; but a government which does not admit of reformation and repen-
tance, must unavoidably involve its subjects in misery;
for the weakness of creatures will always be a source of
error and inconstancy, and a wise Governor, as we must
admit God to be, would suit his government to the
capacity and all other circumstances of the governed;
and instead of inflicting eternal damnation on his offend-
ing children, would rather interchangeably extend his

beneficence with his vindictive punishments, so as to alienate them from sin and wickedness, and incline them to morality ; convincing them from experimental suffering, that sin and vanity are their greatest enemies, and that in God and *moral rectitude* their *dependance* and *true happiness* consists, and by reclaiming them from *wickedness and error*, to the *truth*, and to *the love and practice of virtue*, give them occasion to *glorify* God *for the wisdom and goodness of his government*, and to be ultimately happy under it.   But we are told that the eternal damnation of a part of mankind greatly augments the happiness of the elect, who are represented as being vastly the less numerous, (a diabolical temper of mind in the elect :) besides, how narrow and contractive must such notions of infinite justice and goodness be ?   Who would imagine that the Deity conducts his providence similar to the detestable despots of this world ?   Oh *horrible ?* most *horrible impeachment* of Divine Goodness ! Rather let us exaltedly suppose that God eternally had the ultimate best good of beings generally and individually in his view, with the reward of the virtuous and the punishment of the vicious, and that no other punishment will ever be inflicted, merely *by the divine administration*, but that will *finally* terminate in the best good of the punished, and thereby subserve the great and important ends of the divine government, and be productive of *the restoration and felicity of all finite rational nature.*

The most weighty arguments deducible from the divine nature have been already offered, *to wit*, ultimate end of God, in creation and providence, to do the

greatest possible good and benignity to beings in general,
and consequently, that the great end and design of punishment, in the divine government, must be to reclaim,
restore, and bring revolters from moral rectitude back to
embrace it and to be ultimately happy; as also, that an
eternal punishment, would defeat the very end and
design of punishment itself; and that no good consequences to the punished could arise out of a never ending destruction; but that a total, everlasting, and irre-
parable evil would take place on such part of the moral
creation, as may be thus sentenced to eternal and rem-
ediless perdition; which would argue imperfection either
in the creation, or moral government of God, or in both.

SECTION III.

HUMAN LIBERTY, AGENCY AND ACCOUNTABILITY, CANNOT
BE ATTENDED WITH ETERNAL CONSEQUENCES, EITHER
GOOD OR EVIL.

FROM what has been argued in the foregoing section,
it appears that mankind in this life are not agents of
trial for eternity, but that they will eternally remain
agents of trial. To suppose that our eternal circumstances will be unalterably fixed in happiness or misery,
in consequence of the agency or transactions of this
temporary life, is inconsistent with the moral government of God, and the progressive and retrospective
knowledge of the human mind. God has not put it
into our power to plunge ourselves into eternal woe and
perdition; human liberty is not so extensive, for the

term of human life bears no proportion to eternity succeeding it ; so that there could be no proportion between
a momentary agency, (which is liberty of action,) or
probation, and any supposed eternal consequences of
happiness or misery resulting from it. Our liberty consists in our power of agency, and cannot fall short of,
or exceed it, for liberty is agency itself, or is that by
which agency or action is exerted ; it may be that the
curious would define it, that agency is the effect of lib-
ty, and that liberty is the cause which produces it ;
making a distinction between action and the power of
action ; be it so, yet agency cannot surpass its liberty ;
to suppose otherwise, would be the same as to suppose
agency without the power of agency, or an effect without a cause ; therefore, as our agency does not extend
to consequences of eternal happiness or misery, the
power of that agency, which is liberty, does not. Sufficient it is for virtuous minds, while in this life, that
they keep " *Consciences void of offence towards God
and towards man.*" And that in their commencement
in the succeeding state, they have a retrospective knowledge of their agency in this, and retain a consciousness
of a well spent life. Beings thus possessed of a habit
of virtue, would enjoy a rational felicity beyond the
reach of physical evils which terminate with life ; and in
all rational probability would be advanced in the order
of nature, to a more exalted and sublime manner of
being, knowledge and action, than at present we can
conceive of, where no joys or pains can approach, but of
the mental kind ; in which elevated state virtuous minds
will be able, in a clearer and more copious manner in

this life, to contemplate the superlative beauties of moral fitness ; and with ecstatic satisfaction enjoy it, notwithstanding imperfection and consequently agency, proficiency and trial, of some kind or other, must everlastingly continue with finite minds.

And as to the vicious, who have violated the laws of reason and morality, lived a life of sin and wickedness, and are at as great a remove from a rational happiness as from moral rectitude ; such incorrigible sinners, at their commencing existence in the world of spirits, will undoubtedly have opened to them a tremendous scene of horror, self-condemnation and guilt, with an anguish of mind ; the more so, as no sensual delights can there, (as in this world,) divert the mind from its conscious guilt ; the clear sense of which will be the more pungent, as the mind in that state will be greatly enlarged, and consequently more capaciously susceptible of sorrow, grief, and conscious woe, from a retrospective reflection of a wicked life.

SECTION IV.

OF PHYSICAL EVILS.

PHYSICAL evils are in nature inseparable from animal life, they commenced existence with it, and are its concomitants through life ; so that the same nature which gives being to the one, gives birth to the other also ; the one is not before or after the other, but they are co-existent together, and cotemporaries ; and as they began existence in a necessary dependance on each other, so they terminate together in death and dissolution. This is the original order to which animal nature is subjected, as applied to every species of it. The beasts of the field, the fowls of the air, the fishes of the sea, with reptiles, and all manner of beings, which are possessed with animal life ; nor is pain, sickness, or mortality any part of God's punishment for sin. On the other hand sensual happiness is no part of the reward of virtue : to reward moral actions with a glass of wine or a shoulder of mutton, would be as inadequate, as to measure a triangle with sound, for virtue and vice pertain to the mind, and their merits or demerits have their just effects on the conscience, as has been before evinced : but animal gratifications are common to the human race indiscriminately, and also, to the beasts of the field : and physical evils as promiscuously and universally extend to the whole, so " That there is no knowing good or evil by all that is before us, for all is vanity." It was not among the number of possibles, that animal life should be exempted from mortality : omnipotence itself could not have made it capable of eternalization and indissolubility ; for the self same nature which constitutes animal life, subjects it to decay and dissolution ; so that the one cannot be without the other, any more than there could be a compact number of mountains without vallies, or that I could exist and not exist at the same time, or that God should effect any other contradiction in nature ; all contradictions being equally impossible, inasmuch as they imply an absolute incompatibility with nature and truth ; for nature is predicated on truth, and the same truth which constitutes mountains, made the vallies at the

same time; nor is it possible that they could have a separate existence.   And the same truth which affirms my
existence, denies its negative; so also the same law of
nature, which in truth produceth an animal life and
supports it for a season, wears it out, and in its natural
course reduces it to its original elements again.   The
vegetable world also presents us with a constant aspect
of productions and dissolutions ; and the bustle of elements is beyond all conception ; but the dissolution of
forms is not the dissolution of matter, or the annihilation
of it, nor of the .creation, which exists in all possible
forms and fluxilities ; and it is from such physical alterations of the particles of matter, that animal or vegetable life is produced and destroyed.   Elements afford them
nutrition, and time brings them to maturity, decay and
dissolution ; and in all the prolific production of animal
life, or the productions of those of a vegetative nature,
throughout all their growth, decay and dissolution,
make no addition or diminution of creation ; but eternal
nature continues its never ceasing operations, (which in
most respects are mysterious to us) under the unerring
guidance of the providence of God.
    Animal nature consists of a regular constitution of a
variety of organic parts, which have a particular and
necessary dependance on each other, by the mutual
assistance whereof the whole are animated.   Blood
seems to be the source of life, and it is requisite that
it have a proper circulation from the heart to the extreme
parts of the body, and from thence to the heart again,
that it may repeat its temporary rounds through certain
arteries and veins, which replenish every minutia part

with blood and vital heat ; but the brain is evidently the seat of sensation, which through the nervous system conveys the animal spirits to every part of the body, imparting to it sensation and motion, constituting it a living machine, which could never have been produced, or exercised its respective functions in any other sort of world but this ; which is in a constant series of fluxilities, and which causeth it to produce food for its inhabitants. An unchangeable world could not admit of production or dissolution, but would be identically the same, which would preclude the existence and nutriment of such sensitive creatures as we are. The nutrition extracted from food by the secret aptitudes of the digesting powers (by which mysterious operation it becomes incorporated with the circulating juices, supplying the animal functions with vital heat, strength and vigor) demands a constant flux and reflux of the particles of matter, which is perpetually incorporating with the body, and supplying the place of the superfluous particles that are constantly discharging themselves by insensible prespiration ; supporting, and at the same time, in its ultimate tendency, destroying animal life. Thus it manifestly appears, that the laws of the world in which we live, and the constitution of the animal nature of man, are all but one uniform arrangement of cause and effect ; and as by the course of those laws, animal life is propagated and sustained for a season, so by the operation of the same laws, decay and mortality are the necessary consequences.

2 *

CHAPTER IV.

SECTION I.

SPECULATION ON THE DOCTRINE OF THE DEPRAVITY OF
HUMAN REASON.

In the course of our speculation on Divine Providence we proceed next to the consideration of the doctrine of the depravity of human reason: a doctrine derogatory to the nature of man, and the rank and character of being which he holds in the universe, and which, if admitted to be true overturns knowledge and science and renders learning, instruction and books useless and impertinent; inasmuch as reason, depraved or spoiled, would cease to be reason ; as much as the mind of a raving madman would of course cease to be rational: admitting the depravity of reason, the consequence would unavoidably follow, that as far as it may be supposed to have taken place in the midst of mankind, there could be no judges of it, in consequence of their supposed depravity; for without the exercise of reason, we could not understand what reason is, which would be necessary for us previously to understand, in order to understand what it is not ; or to distinguish it from that which is its reverse.   But for us to have the knowledge of what reason is, and the ability to distinguish it from that which is depraved, or is irrational, is incompatible with the doctrine of the depravity of our reason.   Inasmuch as to understand what reason is, and to distinguish it from that which is marred or spoiled, is the same to all intents and purposes, as to have, exercise and enjoy, the principle of reason itself, which precludes its supposed depravity : so that it is impossible for us to understand what reason is, and at the same time determine that our reason is depraved ; for this would be the same as when we know that we are in possession and exercise of reason, to determine that we are not in possession or exercise of it.

It may be, that some who embrace the doctrine of the depravity of human reason, will not admit that it is wholly and totally depraved, but that it is in a great measure marred or spoiled. But the foregoing arguments are equally applicable to a supposed depravity in parts, as in the whole ; for in order to judge whether reason be depraved in part or not, it would be requisite to have an understanding of what reason may be supposed to have been, previous to its premised depravity ; and to have such a knowledge of it, would be the same as to exercise and enjoy it in its lustre and purity, which would preclude the notion of a depravity in part, as well as in the whole ; for it would be utterly impossible for us to judge of reason undepraved and depraved, but by comparing them together. But for depraved reason to make such a comparison, is contradictory and impossible ; so that, if our reason had been depraved, we could not have had any conception of it any more than a beast. Men of small faculties in reasoning cannot comprehend the extensive reasonings of their superiors, how then can a supposed depraved reason comprehend that reason which is uncorrupted and pure ? To suppose that it could, is the same as to suppose that depraved and undepraved reason is alike, and if so, there needs no further dispute about it.

There is a manifest contradiction in applying the term *depraved* to that ·of reason, the ideas contained in their respective definitions will not admit 'of their association together, as the terms convey heterogeneous ideas ; for reason spoiled, marred, or robbed of its perfection, ceaseth to be rational, and should not be called reason ; inasmuch as it is premised to be depraved, or degenerated from a rational nature ; and in consequence of the deprivation of its nature, should also be deprived of its name, and called subterfuge, or some such like name, which might better define its real character.

Those who invalidate reason, ought seriously to consider, "*whether they argue against reason, with or without reason ; if with reason, then they establish the principle, that they are laboring to dethrone :* " but if they argue without reason, (which, in order to be consistent with themselves, they must do,) they are out of the reach of rational conviction, nor do they deserve a rational argument.

We are told that the knowledge of the depravity of reason, was first communicated to mankind by the immediate inspiration of God. But inasmuch as reason is supposed to be depraved, what principle could there be in the human irrational soul, which could receive or understand the inspiration, or on which it could operate so as to represent to those whom it may be supposed were inspired, the knowledge of the depravity of (their own and mankind's) reason (in general :) for a rational inspiration must consist of rational ideas, which pre-supposes that the minds of those who were inspired, were rational previous to such inspiration, which would be a downright contradiction to the inspiration itself; the import of which was to teach the knowledge of the depravity of human reason, which without reason could not be understood, and with reason it would be understood, that the inspiration was false.

Will any advocates for the depravity of reason suppose, that inspiration ingrafts or superadds the essence of reason itself to the human mind? Admitting it to be so, yet such inspired persons could not understand any thing of reason, before the reception of such supposed inspiration; nor would such a premised inspiration prove to its possessors or receivers, that their reason had ever been depraved. All that such premised inspired persons could understand, or be conscious of, respecting reason, would be after the inspiration may be supposed to have taken effect, and made them rational beings, and then instead of being taught by inspiration, that their reason had been previously depraved, they could have had no manner of consciousness of the existence or exercise of it, until the impairing the principle of it by the supposed energy of inspiration; nor could such supposed inspired persons- communicate the knowledge of such a premised revelation to others of the species, who for want of a rational nature, could not be supposed, *on this position,* to be able to receive the impressions of reason.

That there are degrees in the knowledge of rational beings, and also in their capacities to acquire it, cannot be disputed, as it is so very obvious among mankind. But in all the retrospect gradations from the exalted reasonings of a Locke or a Newton, down to the lowest exercise of it among the species, still it is reason, and not depraved; for a less degree of reason by no means implies a depravity of it, nor does the imparting of reason argue its depravity, for what remains of reason, or rather of the exercise of it, is reason still. But there is not, and cannot be such a thing as depraved reason, for that which is rational is so, and for that reason cannot be depraved, whatever its degree of exercise may be supposed to be.

A blow on the head, or fracture of the cranium, as also palsies and many other casualties that await our sensorium, retard, and in some cases wholly prevent the exercise of reason for a longer or shorter period; and sometimes through the stage of human life; but in such instances as these, reason is not depraved, but ceases in a greater or less degree, or perhaps wholly ceases its rational exertions or operations; by reason of the breaches or disorders of the organs of sense, but in such instances, wherein the organs become rectified, and the senses recover their usefulness, the exercise of reason returns, free from any blemish or depravity. For the cessation of the exercise of reason, by no means depraves it.

From what has been argued on this subject, in this and the preceding chapters, it appears that reason is not and cannot be depraved, but that it bears a likeness to divine reason, is of the same kind, and in its own nature as uniform as truth, which is the test of it; though in the divine essence, it is eternal and infinite, but in man it is eternal only as it respects their immortality, and finite as it respects capaciousness. Such people as can be prevailed upon to believe, that their reason is depraved, may easily be led by the nose, and duped into superstition at the pleasure of those in whom they confide, and there remain from generation to generation : for when they throw by the law of reason *the only one* which God gave them to direct them in their speculations and duty, they are exposed to ignorant or insiduous teachers, and also to their own irregular passions, and to the folly and enthusiasm of those about them, which nothing but reason can prevent or restrain : nor is it a rational supposition that the commonality of mankind would ever have mistrusted that their reason was depraved, had they not been told so, and it is whispered about, that the first insinuation of it was from the Priests; (though the Armenian Clergymen in the circle of my acquaintance have exploded the doctrine.) Should we admit the depravity of reason, it would equally affect the priesthood, or any other teachers of that doctrine, with the rest of mankind; but for depraved creatures to receive and give credit to a depraved doctrine, started and taught by depraved creatures, is the greatest weakness and folly imaginable, and comes nearer a proof of the doctrine of total depravity, than any arguments which have been advanced in support of it.

SECTION II.

CONTAINING A DISQUISITION OF THE LAW OF NATURE, AS IT
RESPECTS THE MORAL SYSTEM, INTERSPERSED WITH
OBSERVATIONS ON SUBSEQUENT RELIGIONS.

THAT mankind are by nature endowed with sensation
and reflection, from which results the power of reason
and understanding, will not be disputed. The senses
are well calculated to make discoveries of external objects
and to communicate those notices, or simple images of
things to the mind, with all the magnificent simplicity
of nature, which opens an extensive field of contemplation to the understanding, enabling the mind to examine
into the natural causes and consequences of things, and
to investigate the knowledge of moral good and evil,
from which, together with the power of agency, results
the human conscience. This is the original of moral
obligation and accountability, which is called natural
religion ; for without the understanding of truth from
falsehood, and right from wrong, which is the same as
justice from injustice, and a liberty of agency, which is
the same as a power of proficiency in either moral good
or evil : mankind would not be rational or accountable
creatures. Undoubtedly it was the ultimate design of
our Creator, in giving us being, and furnishing us with
those noble compositions of mental powers and sensitive
aptitudes, that we should, in, by, and with that nature,
serve and honor him ; and with those united capacities, search out and understand our duty to him, and to
one another, with the ability of practising the same as

far as may be necessary for us in this life. To object against the sufficiency of natural religion, to effect the best ultimate good of mankind, would be derogating from the wisdom, goodness, and justice of God, who in the course of his providence to us, has adopted it: besides, if natural religion may be supposed to be deficient, what security can we have that any subsequently revealed religion should not be so also ? For why might not a second religion from God be as insufficient or defective as a first religion may be supposed to be ? From hence we infer that if natural religion be insufficient to dictate mankind in the way of their duty and make them ultimately happy, there is an end to religion in general. But as certain as God is perfect in wisdom and goodness, natural religion is sufficient and complete ; and having had the divine approbation, and naturally resulting from a rational nature, is as universally promulgated to mankind as reason itself. But to the disadvantage of the claim of all subsequent religions, *called revelations, whether denominated inspired, external, supernatural, or what not,* they came too late into the world to be essential to the well being of mankind, or to point out to them the only way to heaven and everlasting blessedness : inasmuch as for the greatest part of mankind who have ever lived in this world, have departed this life previous to the eras and promulgations of such revelations. Besides, those subsequent revelations to the law of nature, began as human traditions have ever done in very small circumferences, in the respective parts of the world where they have been inculcated, and made their progress, as time, chance, and opportunity presented. Does this look like the contrivance of heaven, and the only way of salvation? Or is it not more like this world and the contrivance of man? Undoubtedly the great parent of mankind laid a just and sufficient foundation of salvation for every one of them; for otherwise such of them, who may be supposed not to be thus provided for would not have whereof to glorify God for their being, but on the contrary would have just matter of complaint against his providence or moral government for involuntarily necessitating them into a wretched and miserable existence, and that without end or remedy: which would be ascribing to God a more extensive injustice than is possible to be charged on the most barbarous despots that ever were among mankind.

But to return to our speculations on the law of nature. That this divine Law surpasses all positive institutions, that have ever been ushered into the world since its creation as much as the wisdom and goodness of God exceeds that of man, is beautifully illustrated in the following quotation: " But it may be said what is virtue? It is the faithful discharge of those obligations which reason dictates. And what is wisdom itself, but a portion of intelligence? with which the creator has furnished us, in order to direct us in our duty? It may be further asked, what is this duty? whence does it result? and by what law is it prescribed? I answer that the law which prescribed it is the immutable will of God; to which right reason obliges us to conform ourselves, and in this conformity virtue consists. No law which has commenced since the creation, or which may ever cease to be in force, can constitute virtue; for before the existence of such a law, mankind could not be bound to observe it; but they were certainly under an obligation to be virtuous from the beginning. Princes may make laws and repeal them, but they can neither make nor destroy virtue, and how indeed should they be able to do what is impossible to the Deity himself? Virtue being as immutable in its nature as the divine will which is the ground of it.*

A Prince may command his subjects to pay taxes or subsidies, may forbid them to export certain commodities, or to introduce those of a foreign country. The faithful observance of these laws make obedient subjects, but does not make virtuous men; and would any one seriously think himself possessed of a virtue the more for not having dealt in painted calico; or if the Prince should by his authority abrogate these laws, would any one say he had abrogated virtue? It is thus with all positive laws; they all had a beginning — are all liable to exceptions, and may be dispensed with and even abolished. That law alone which is engraven on our hearts by the hand of our creator, is unchangeable and of universal and eternal obligation. The law, says Cicero, is not a human invention, nor an arbitrary political institution, it is in its nature eternal and of universal obligation. The

---

* Virtue did not derive its nature merely from the omnipotent will of God, but also from the eternal truth and moral fitness of things; which was the eternal reason why they were eternally approved of by God, and immutably established by him, to be what they are; and so far as our duty is connected with those eternal measures of moral fitness, or we are able to act on them, we give such actions or habits the name of virtue or morality. But when we, in writing or conversation, say that virtue is grounded on the divine will, we should at the same time include in the complex idea of it, that the divine will which constituted virtue, was eternally and infinitely reasonable.

violence Tarquin offered to Lucretia, was a breach of that
eternal law, and though the Romans at that time might
have no written law which condemned such kind of
crimes, his offence was not the less heinous; for this law
of reason did not then begin, when it was first committed
to writing; its original is as ancient as the divine mind.
For the true, primitive and supreme law, is no other than
the unerring reason of the great Jupiter. And in another place he says, this law is founded in nature, it is universal, immutable, and eternal, it is subject to no change
from any difference of place, or time, it extends invaria-
bly to all ages and nations, like the sovereign dominion
of that Being, who is author of it."

The promulgation of this supreme law to creatures, is
co-extensive and co-existent with reason, and binding on
all intelligent beings in the universe; and is that eternal
rule of fitness, as applicable to God, by which the creator of all things conducts his infinitude of providence,
and by which he governs the moral system of being, according to the absolute perfection of his nature. From
hence we infer, that admitting those subsequent revelations, which have more or less obtained credit in the world,
as the inspired laws of God, to be consonant to the laws
of nature, yet they could be considered as none other but
mere transcripts therefrom, promulgated to certain favorite nations, when at the same time all mankind was favored with the original.

The moral precepts contained in Moses' decalogue to
the people of Israel, was previously known to every nation under heaven, and in all probability by them as much
practised as by the tribes of Israel. Their keeping the

seventh day of the week as a sabbath was an arbitrary imposition of Moses, (as many other of his edicts were) and not included in the law of nature. But as to such laws of his, or those of any other legislator, which are morally fit, agree with, and are a part of the natural law, as for instance; " Thou shalt not covet," or " kill." These positive injunctions cannot add anything to the law of nature, inasmuch as it contains an entire and perfect system of morality ; nor can any positive injunctions or commands enforce the authority of it, or confer any additional moral obligation on those to whom they are given to obey ; the previous obligation of natural religion, having ever been as binding as reason can possibly conceive of, or the order and constitution of the moral rectitude of things, as resulting from God, can make it to be.

To illustrate the argument of the obligatory nature of the natural law let us reverse the commandments of the decalogue, by premising that Moses had said thou shalt covet ; thou shalt steal and murder ; would any one conclude, that the injunctions would have been obligatory ? surely they would not, for a positive command to violate the law of nature could not be binding on any rational being. How then came the injunctions of Moses, or any others, to be binding in such cases, in which they coincide with the law of nature ? We answer, merely in consequence of the obligatory sanctions of the natural law, which does not at all depend on the authority of Moses or of any other legislator, short of him who is eternal and infinite ; nor is it possible that the Jews, who adhere to the law of Moses, should be under greater obligation to the moral law, than the Japanese ; or the Christians than the Chinese ; for the same God extends the same moral government over universal rational nature, independent of Popes, Priests and Levites.   But with respect to all mere positive institutions, injunctions, rites and ceremonies, that do not come within the jurisdiction of the law of nature, they are political matters, and may be enacted, perpetuated, dispensed with, abolished, re-enacted, compounded or diversified, as conveniency, power, opportunity, inclination, or interest, or all together may dictate ; inasmuch as they are not founded on any stable or universal principle of reason, but change with the customs, fashions, traditions and revolutions of the world ; having no centre of attraction, but interest, power and advantages of a temporary nature.

Was the creator and governor of the universe to erect a particular academy of arts and sciences in this world, under his immediate inspection, with tutors rightly organized, and intellectually qualified to carry on the business of teaching, it might like other colleges, (and possibly in a superior manner,) instruct its scholars.   But that God should have given a revelation of his will to mankind, as his law, and to be continued to the latest posterity as such, which is premised to be above the capacity of their understanding, is contradictory and in its own nature impossible.   Nor could a revelation to mankind, which comes within the circle of their knowledge, be edifying or instructing to them, for it is a contradiction to call that which is above my comprehension, or that which I already, (from natural sagacity) understand, a revelation to me: to tell me, or inspire me, with the knowledge of that which I knew before, would reveal nothing to me,

and to reveal that to me which is supernatural or above
my comprehension, is contradictory and impossible. But
the truth of the matter is, that mankind are restricted by
the law of nature to acquire knowledge or science progressively, as before argued. From which we infer the
impropriety, and consequently the impossibility of God's
having ever given us any manuscript copy of his eternal
law : for that to reveal it at first would bring it on a
level with the infancy of knowledge then in the world,
or (fishermen, shepherds, and illiterate people could not
have understood it,) which would have brought it so low
that it could not be instructive or beneficial to after generations in their progressive advances in science and wisdom.

CHAPTER V.

SECTION I.

ARGUMENTATIVE REFLECTIONS ON SUPERNATURAL AND MYSTERIOUS REVELATION IN GENERAL.

THERE is not anything which has contributed so much
to delude mankind in religious matters, as mistaken apprehensions concerning supernatural inspiration or revelation ; not considering that all true religion originates
from reason, and can no otherwise be understood but by
the exercise and improvement of it ; therefore they are
apt to confuse their minds with such inconsistencies. In
the subsequent reasonings on this subject, we shall argue
against supernatural revelation in general, which will
comprehend the doctrine of inspiration or immediate illumination of the mind. And first — we will premise, that

a revelation consists of an assemblage of rational ideas, intelligibly arranged and understood by those to whom it may be supposed to be revealed, for otherwise it could not exist in their minds as such. To suppose a revelation, void of rationality or understanding, or of communicating rational intelligence to those, to whom it may be supposed to be given, would be a contradiction; for that it could contain nothing except it were unintelligibleness which would be the same as to reveal and not to reveal; therefore, a revelation must consist of an assemblage of rational ideas, intelligibly communicated to those who are supposed to have been the partakers or receivers of it from the first supposed inspiration, down to this or any other period of time. But such a revelation as this, could be nothing more or less than a transcript of the law of nature, predicated on reason, and would be no more supernatural, than the reason of man may be supposed to be. The simple definition of supernatural is, that which is " beyond or above the powers of nature," which never was or can be understood by mankind; the first promulgators of revelation not excepted; for such revelation, doctrine, precept or instruction only, as comes within the powers of our nature, is capable of being apprehended, contemplated or understood by us, and such as does not, is to us incomprehensible and unknown, and consequently cannot for us compose any part of revelation.

The author of human nature impressed it with certain sensitive aptitudes and mental powers, so that apprehension, reflection or understanding could no otherwise be exerted or produced in the compound nature of man, but in the order prescribed by the creator. It would therefore be a contradiction in nature, and consequently impossible for God to inspire, infuse, or communicate the apprehension, reflection or understanding of any thing whatever into human nature, out of, above, or beyond the natural aptitudes, and mental powers of that nature, which was of his own production and constitution ; for it would be the same as to inspire, infuse, or reveal apprehension, reflection or understanding, to that which is not ; inasmuch as out of, beyond or above the powers of nature, there could be nothing to operate upon, as a prerequisite principle to receive the inspiration or infusion of the revelation, which might therefore as well be inspired into, or revealed to nonentity, as to man. For the essence of man is that, which we denominate to be his nature, out of or above which he is as void of sensation, apprehension, reflection and understanding, as nonentity may be supposed to be ; therefore such revelation as is adapted to the nature and capacity of man, and comes within his powers of perception and understanding, is the only revelation, which he is able to receive from God or man. Supernatural revelation is as applicable to beasts, birds and fishes, as it is to us ; for neither we nor they are capable of being acted upon supernaturally, as all the possible exertions and operations of nature, which respect the natural or moral world, are truly natural. Nor does God deviate from his rectitude of nature in matters of inspiration, revelation or instruction to the moral world, any more than in that of his government of the natural.

The infinitude of the wisdom of God's creation, providence and moral government will eternally remain supernatural to all finite capacities, and for that very reason

3

we can never arrive to the comprehension of it, in any
state of being and improvement whatever; inasmuch as
progression can never attain to that which is infinite, so
that an eternal proficiency in knowledge could not be supernatural, but on the other hand would come within the
limits and powers of our nature, for otherwise such proficiency would be impossible to us; nor is this infinite
knowledge of God supernatural to him, for that his perfection is also infinite. But if we could break over the
limits of our capacity, so as to understand any one supernatural thing, which is above or beyond the power of our
natures, we might by that rule as well understand all
things, and thus by breaking over the confines of finite
nature and the rank of being which we hold in the universe, comprehend the knowledge of infinity. From
hence we infer, that every kind and degree ef apprehension, reflection and understanding, which we can attain
to in any state of improvement whatever, is no more supernatural than the nature of man, from whence perception and understanding is produced, may be supposed to
be so : nor has or could God Almighty ever have revealed himself to mankind in any other way or manner, but
what is truly natural.

SECTION II.

CONTAINING OBSERVATIONS ON THE PROVIDENCE AND AGEN-
CY OF GOD, AS IT RESPECTS THE NATURAL AND MORAL
WORLD, WITH STRICTURES ON REVELATION IN GENERAL.

THE idea of a God we infer from our experimental dependence on something superior to ourselves in wisdom,
power and goodness, which we call God ; our senses discover to us the works of God which we call nature, and
which is a manifest demonstration of his invisible essence.
Thus it is from the works of nature that we deduce the
knowledge of a God, and not because we have, or can
have any immediate knowledge of, or revelation from
him.   But on the other hand, all our understanding of,
or intelligence from God, is communicated to us by the
intervention of natural causes, (which is not of the divine
essence ;) this we denominate to be natural revelation, for
that it is mediately made known to us by our senses, and
from our sensations of external objects in general, so that
all and every part of the universe, of which we have any
conception, is exterior from the nature or essence of God ;
nor is it in the nature of things possible for us to receive,
or for God to communicate any inspiration or revelation
to us, but by the instrumentality of intermediate causes,
as has been before observed.   Therefore all our notions
of the immediate interposition of divine illuminations, inspiration, or infusion of ideas or revelations into our
minds, is mere enthusiasm and deception ; for that neither the divine mind, nor those of any finite intelligences
can make any representation to, or impression on our ex-

ternal senses without the assistance of some adequate, intermediate cause. The same is the case between man
and man, or with mankind in general ; we can no otherwise hold a correspondence but by the aptitude, and
through the medium of our senses. Since this is the
only possible way in nature by which we can receive any
notices, perceptions, or intelligence from God or man.

Nothing can be more unreasonable than to suppose,
because God is infinitely powerful, that he can therefore
inspire or infuse perception, reflection or revelation into
the mind of man in such a way or manner as is incompatible with the aptitudes and powers of their nature :
such a revelation would be as impossible to be revealed
by God, as by a mere creature. For though it is a maxim of truth, "That with God all things are possible,"
yet it should be considered, that contradictions, and consequently impossibilities are not comprehended in the definition of things, but are diametrically the reverse of them,
as may be seen in the definition of the word THINGS, to
wit : "whatever is." There is no contradiction in nature or truth, which comprehends or contains all things,
therefore the maxim is just, " That with God all things
are possible," viz : all things in nature are possible with
God ; but contradictions are falsehoods which have no
positive existence, but are the negatives to THINGS, or to
nature, which comprehends, "Whatever is ;" so that
contradictions are opposed to nature and truth, and are
no THINGS, but the chimeras of weak, unintelligent minds
who make false application of things to persons, or ascribe such powers, qualities, dispositions and aptitudes to
things as nature never invested them with ; such are our

deluded notions of the immediate operations of the holy
spirit, or of any mere spirit, on our minds independent
of the intervention of some adequate, natural or intermediate cause. To make a triangle four square, or to make
a variety of mountains contiguously situated, without vallies, or to give existence to a thing and not to give existence to it at the same time, or to reveal anything to us
incompatible with our capacity of receiving the perception of it, pertains to those negatives to nature and truth,
and are not things revealed, nor have they any positive
existence as has been before argued ; for they are inconsistent with themselves, and the relations and effects
which they are supposed to have upon and with each other. It derogates nothing from the power and absolute
perfection of God that he cannot make both parts of a
contradiction to be true.

But let us reverse the position concerning revelation,
and premise that it is accommodated to our capacity of
receiving and understanding it, and in this case it would
be natural, and therefore possible for us to receive and
understand it ; for the same truth which is predicated on
the sufficiency of our capacity to receive and understand
a revelation, affirms at the same time the possibility of
our receiving and understanding it. But to suppose that
God can make both parts of a contradiction to be true, to
reveal and not reveal, would be the same as ascribing a
falsehood to him and to call it by the name of power.

That God can do anything and everything, that is consonant to his moral perfections, and which does not imply a contradiction to the nature of the things themselves,
and the essential relation which they bear to each other,

none will dispute. But to suppose, that inasmuch as
God is all-powerful, he can therefore do everything,
which we in our ignorance of nature or of moral fitness
may ascribe to him, without understanding, whether it
is either consonant to moral rectitude, or to the nature of
the things themselves, and the immutable relations and
connections which they bear to each other, or not, is great
weakness and folly.   That God cannot in the exercise of
his providence or moral government, counteract the perfections of his nature, or do any manner of injustice, is
manifestly certain ; nor is it possible for God to effect a
contradiction in the natural world, any more than in the
moral.   The impossibility of the one results from the
\ moral perfections of God, and the impossibility of the
other from the immutable properties, qualities, relations
and nature of the things themselves, as in the instances
of the mountains, vallies, &c., before alluded to, and in
numberless other such like cases.

Admitting a revelation to be from God, it must be
allowed to be infallible, therefore those to whom it may
be supposed to have been first revealed from God, must
have had an infallible certainty of their inspiration : so
likewise the rest of mankind, to whom it is proposed as
a Divine Law, or rule of duty, should have an infallible
certainty, that its first promulgators were thus truly
inspired by the immediate interposition of the spirit of
God, and that the revelation has been preserved through
all the changes and revolutions of the world to their
time, and that the copies extant present them with its
original inspiration and unerring composure, or are perfectly agreeable to it.   All this we must have an infalli-

ble certainty of, or we fail of an infallible certainty of revelation, and are liable to be imposed upon by impostors, or by ignorant and insidious teachers, whose interest it may be to obtrude their own systems on the world for infallible truth, as in the instance of Mahomet.

But let us consult our own constitutions and the world in which we live, and we shall find that inspiration is, in the very nature of things, impossible to be understood by us, and of consequence not in fact true. What certainty can we have of the agency of the divine mind on ours? Or how can we distinguish the supposed divine illuminations or ideas from those of our own which are natural to us? In order for us to be certain of the interposition of immediate divine inspiration in our minds we must be able to analyze, distinguish, and distinctly separate the premised divine reflections, illuminations or inspiration from our own natural cogitations, for otherwise we should be liable to mistake our reflections and reasonings for God's inspiration, as is the case with enthusiasts, or fanatics, and thus impose on ourselves, and obtrude our romantic notions on mankind, as God's revelation.

None will, it is presumed, pretend that the natural reflections of our minds are dictated by the immediate agency of the divine spirit; for if they were thus dictated, they would be of equal authority with any supposed inspired revelation. How then shall we be able to distinguish or understand our natural perceptions, reflections or reasonings, from any premised immediately inspired ones? Should God make known to us, or to any of us, a revelation by a voice, and that in a language

which we understand, and admitting that the propositions, doctrines, or subject matter of it, should not exceed
our capacity, we could understand it the same as we do
in conversation with one another ; but this would be an
external and natural revelation, in which God is supposed to make use of language, grammar, logic and
sound, *alias* of intermediate causes, in order to communicate or reveal it, which would differ as much from an
immediately inspired revelation, as this book may be
supposed to do; for the very definition of immediate
inspiration precludes all natural or immediate causes.
That God is eternally perfect in knowledge, and therefore knows all things, not by succession or by parts, as
we understand things by degrees, has been already
evinced ; nevertheless all truth, which we arrive at the
understanding of, accords with the divine omniscience,
but we do not come at the comprehension of things by
immediate infusion, or inspiration, but from reasoning ;
for we cannot see or hear God think or reason any more
than man, nor are our senses susceptible of a mere mental communion with him, nor is it in nature possible for
the human mind to receive any instantaneous or immediate illuminations or ideas from the divine spirit (as
before argued,) but we must illuminate and improve our
minds by a close application to the study of nature,
through the series whereof God has been pleased to
reveal himself to man, so that we may truly say, that
the knowledge of nature is the revelation of God.   In
this there can be no delusion, it is natural, and could
come from none other but God.

Unless we could do this, we should compound them

together at a venture, and form a revelation like Nebuchadnezzar's idol, " partly iron and partly clay," *alias* partly divine and partly human. The Apostle Paul informs !us, that sometimes he " spake, and not the Lord," and at other times speaks doubtfully about the matter, saying, " and I THINK also that I have the spirit of God," and if he was at a loss about his inspiration, well may we be distrustful of it. From the foregoing speculations on the subject of supernatural inspiration, it appears, that there are insuperable difficulties in a mere mental discourse with the divine spirit; it is what we are unacquainted with, and the law of our nature forbids it. Our method of conversation is vocal, or by writing, or by some sort of external symbols which are the mediate ground of it, and we are liable to errors and mistakes in this natural and external way of correspondence; but when we have the vanity to rely on dreams and visions to inform ourselves of things, or attempt to commune with invisible finite beings, or with the holy spirit, our deceptions, blunders and confusions are increased to fanaticism itself; as the diverse supposed influence of the spirit, on the respective sectaries, even among Christians, may witness, as it manifestly, in their empty conceit of it, conforms to every of their traditions. Which evinces, that the whole bustle of it is mere enthusiasm, for was it dictated by the spirit of truth and uniformity itself, it would influence all alike, however zealots persuade themselves and one another that they have supernatural communion with the Holy Ghost, from whence they tell us they derive their notions of religion, and in their frenzy are proof against reason and argument,

3 *

which if we tender them, they tell us, that it is carnal
and depraved reasoning, but that their teachings are
immediately from God, and then proceed to vent upon
us all the curses and punishments, which are written in
the book of the law.

There has in the different parts and ages of the world,
been a multiplicity of immediate and wonderful discoveries, said to have been made to godly men of old by the
special illumination or supernatural inspiration of God,
every of which have, in doctrine, precept and instruction,
been essentially different from each other, which are consequently as repugnant to truth, as the diversity of the
influence of the spirit on the multiplicity of sectaries
has been represented to be.

These facts, together with the premises and inferences
as already deduced, are too evident to be denied, and
operate conclusively against immediate or supernatural
revelation in general ; nor will such revelation hold good
in theory any more than in practice. Was a revelation
to be made known to us, it must be accommodated to our
external senses, and also to our reason, so that we could
come at the perception and understanding of it, the same
as we do to that of things in general. We must perceive by our senses, before we can reflect with the mind.
Our sensorium is that essential medium between the
divine and human mind, through which God reveals to
man the knowledge of nature, and is our only door of
correspondence with God or with man.

A premised revelation, adapted to our external senses,
would enable our mental powers to reflect upon, examine
into, and understand it. Always provided nevertheless,

that the subject matter of such revelation, or that of the doctrines, precepts or injunctions therein contained, do not exceed our reason, but are adapted to it as well as to our external senses.

To suppose that God, merely from his omnipotence, without the intervention of some adequate intermediate cause could make use of sound, or grammatical and logical language, or of writing, so as to correspond with us, or to reveal any thing to us, would run into the same sort of absurdity, which we have already confuted; for it is the same as to suppose an effect without a suitable or a proportionable cause, or an effect without a cause; whereas, effects must have adequate causes or they could not be produced. God is the self-existent and eternal cause of all things, but the eternal cause can no otherwise operate on the eternal succession of causes and effects, but by the mutual operation of those causes on each other, according to the fixed laws of nature. For as we have frequently observed before that of all possible systems, infinite wisdom comprehended the best; and infinite goodness and power must have adopted and perfected it; and being once established into an ordinance of nature, it could not be deviated from by God: for that it would necessarily imply a manifest imperfection in God, either in its eternal establishment, or in its premised subsequent alteration, which will be more particularly considered in the next chapter.

To suppose that Almighty power could produce a voice, language, grammar, or logic, so as to communicate a revelation to us, without some sort of organic or instrumentated machine or intermediate vehicle, or adequate constituted external cause, would imply a contradiction to the order of nature and consequently to the perfection of God, who established it ; therefore, provided God has ever given us any particular revelation, we must suppose, that he has made use of a regular and natural constituted and mediate ,cause, comprehended in the external order of nature, rightly fitted and abilitated to make use of the vocal power of language, which comprises that of characters, orthography, grammar and logic, all which must have been made use of, in communicating a sup- posed revelation to mankind, which forecloses inspira- tion.

Furthermore, this heavenly dictating voice should have been accommodated to all languages, grammars and logi- cal ways of speaking, in which a revelation may have been divulged, as it would be needful to have been con- tinued from the beginning to every receiver, compiler, translator, printer, commentator on and teacher of such revelation, in order to have informed mankind in every instance, wherein at any time they may have been im- posed upon by any spurious adulterations or interpola- tions, and how it was in the original. These, with the refinements of languages and translations, are a summary of the many ways, wherein we may have been deceived by giving credit to antiquated written revelation, which would need a series of miracles to promulgate and per- petuate it in the world free from mistakes and frauds of one kind or other, and which leads me to the considera- tion of the doctrine of miracles.

CHAPTER · VI.

SECTION I.

OF MIRACLES.

PREVIOUS to the arguments concerning miracles, it is requisite that we give a definition of them, that the arguments may be clearly opposed to the doctrine of miracles, the reality of which we mean to negative ; so that we do not dispute about matters in which we are all agreed, but that we may direct our speculations to the subject matter or essence of the controversy.

We will therefore premise, that miracles are opposed to, and counteract the laws of nature, or that they imply an absolute alteration in either a greater or less degree, the eternal order, disposition and tendency of it ; this, we conclude, is a just definition of miraculousness, and is that for which the advocates for miracles contend, in their defining of miracles. For if they were supposed to make no alteration in the natural order of things, they could have no positive existence, but the laws of nature would produce their effects, which would preclude their reality, and render them altogether fictitious, inasmuch as their very existence is premised to consist in their opposition to, and alteration of the laws of nature : so that if this is not effected, miracles can have no positive existence, any more than nonentity itself; therefore, if in the course of the succeeding arguments, we should evince that the laws of nature have not and cannot be perverted, altered or suspended, it will foreclose miracles by making all things natural. Having thus defined miracles, and stated the dispute, we proceed to the arguments.

Should there ever have been a miraculous suspension and alteration of the laws of nature, God must have been the immediate author of it, as no finite beings may be supposed to be able to alter those laws or regulations, which were established by omnipotent power and infinite perfection, and which nothing short of such power and perfection can perpetuate. This then is the single point at issue, viz: whether God has, or can, consistent with his nature as God, in any instance whatever, alter or deviate from the laws, with which he has eternally impressed the universe, or not.

1.– To suppose that God should subvert his laws, (which is the same as changing them) would be to suppose him to be mutable; for that it would necessarily imply, either that their eternal establishment was imperfect, or 2.–that a premised alteration thereof is so. To alter or change that which is absolutely perfect, would necessarily make it cease to be perfect, inasmuch as perfection could not be altered for the better, but for the worse, and consequently an alteration could not meet with the divine approbation; which terminates the issue of the matter in question against miracles, and authorizes us to deduce the following conclusive inference, to wit: that Almighty God, having eternally impressed the universe with a certain system of laws, for the same eternal reason that they were infinitely perfect and best, they could never admit of the least alteration, but are as unchangable, in their nature, as God their immutable author. To form the foregoing argument into syllogisms, it would be thus : —

God is perfect — the laws of nature were established by God; therefore, the laws of nature are perfect.

But admitting miracles, the syllogism should be thus : —

The laws of nature were in their eternal establishment perfect ; — the laws of nature have been altered ; therefore, the alteration of the laws of nature is imperfect.

Or thus : *the laws of nature have been altered ; — the alteration has been for the better ; therefore, the eternal establishment thereof was imperfect.*

Thus it appears, from a syllogistical as well as other methods of reasoning, that provided we admit of miracles, which are synonymous to the alterations of nature, we by so doing derogate from the perfection of God, either in his eternal constitution of nature, or in a supposed subsequent miraculous alteration of it, so that take the argument either way, and it preponderates against miracles.

Furthermore, was it possible, that the eternal order of nature should have been imperfect, there would be an end to all perfection. For God might be as imperfect in any supposed miraculous works, as in those of nature ; nor could we ever have any security under his natural or moral government, if they were liable to change ; for mutability is but another term for imperfection, or is inseparably connected with it.

God, the great architect of nature, has so constructed its machinery, that it never needs to be altered or rectified. In vain we endeavor to search out the hidden mystery of a perpetual motion, in order to copy nature, for after all our researches we must be contented with such mechanism as will run down, and need rectification again; but the machine of the universe admits of no rectification, but continues its never ceasing operations, under the unerring guidance of the providence of God. Human architects make and unmake things, and alter them as their invention may dictate, and experience may determine to be most convenient and best. But that mind, which is infinitely perfect, gains nothing by experience, but surveys the immense universality of things, with all their possible relations, fitnesses and unfitnesses, of both a natural or moral kind, with one comprehensive view.

SECTION II.

A SUCCESSION OF KNOWLEDGE, OR OF THE EXERTION OF POWER IN GOD, INCOMPATIBLE WITH HIS OMNISCIENCE OR OMNIPOTENCE, AND THE ETERNAL AND INFINITE DISPLAY OF DIVINE POWER FORECLOSES ANY SUBSEQUENT EXERTION OF IT MIRACULOUSLY.

THAT creation is as eternal and infinite as God, has been argued in chapter second; and that there could be no succession in creation, or the exertion of the power of God, in perfecting the boundless work, and in impressing the universe with harmonious laws, perfectly well adapted to their design, use and end.

First. These arguments may be further illustrated, and the evidence of the being of a God more fully exhibited, from the following considerations, to wit: dependent beings and existences must be dependent on some being or cause that is independent, for dependent beings, or existences, could not exist independently ; and, in as much as by retrospectively tracing the order of the succession of causes, we cannot include in our numeration the independent cause, as the several successive causes still depend on their preceding cause, and that preceding cause on the cause preceding it, and so on beyond numerical calculations, we are therefore obliged (as rational beings) to admit an independent cause of all things, for that a mere succession of dependent causes cannot constitute an independent cause ; and from hence we are obliged to admit a self-existent and sufficient cause of all things, for otherwise it would be dependent and insufficient to have given existence to itself, or to have been the efficient cause of all things.

Having thus established the doctrine of a self-sufficient, self-existent, and consequently all-powerful cause of all things, we ascribe an eternal existence to this cause of all causes and effects, whom we call God. And, inasmuch, as from the works of nature it is manifest, that God is possessed of almighty power, we from hence infer his eternal existence. Since his premised existence at (and not before) any given era, would be a conclusive objection to the omnipotency of his power, that he had not existed before, or eternally. For as God is a being self-sufficient, self-existent, and almighty, (as before argued) his power must apply to his own existence as well as to the existence of things in general, and therefore, if he did not eternally exist, it must be because he had not the almighty power of existence in himself, and if so, he never could have existed at all ; so that God must have eternally existed or not have existed at all ; and inasmuch as the works of nature evince his positive existence, and as he could not be dependent on the power, will, or pleasure of any other being but himself for his existence, and as an existence in time would be a contradiction to his almighty power of self-existency, that he had not eternally existed ; therefore, his existence must have been (in truth) eternal.

Although it is to us incomprehensible that any being could be self-existent or eternal (which is synonymous,) yet we can comprehend, that any being that is not self-existent and eternal and dependent and finite, and consequently not a God.　Hence we infer, that though we cannot comprehend the true God (by reason of our own finiteness,) yet [we can negatively comprehend that an imperfect being cannot be God.　A dependent being is finite, and therefore imperfect, and consequently not a God.　A being that has existed at a certain era (and not before) is a limited one, for beyond his era he was not, and therefore finite, and consequently not a God.　Therefore, that being only who is self-existent, infinitely perfect and eternal, is the true God : and if eternally and infinitely perfect, there must have been an eternal and infinite display, and if an eternal and infinite display, it could be nothing short of an eternal and infinite creation and providence.

As to the existence of a God, previous to Moses's era of the first day's work, he does not inform us.　The first notice he gives us of a God was of his laborious working by the day, a theory of creation (as I should think) better calculated for the servile Israelitish *Brick-makers,* than for men of learning and science in these modern mes.

SECTION III.

RARE AND WONDERFUL PHENOMENA NO EVIDENCE OF MIR-
ACLES, NOR ARE DIABOLICAL SPIRITS ABLE TO EFFECT
THEM, OR SUPERSTITIOUS TRADITIONS TO CONFIRM THEM,
NOR CAN ANCIENT MIRACLES PROVE RECENT REVELATIONS.

COMETS, earthquakes, volcanoes, and northern lights (in the night,) with many other extraordinary phenomena or appearances intimidate weak minds, and are by them thought to be miraculous, although they undoubtedly have their proper natural causes, which have been in a great measure discovered. Jack-with-a-lantern is a frightful appearance to some people, but not so much as the imaginary spectre. But of all the scarecrows which have made human nature tremble, the devil has been chief; his family is said to be very numerous, consisting of "legions," with which he has kept our world in a terrible uproar. To tell of all the feats and diabolical tricks, which this infernal family is said to have played upon our race, would compose a volume of an enormous size. All the magicians, necromancers, wizards, witches, conjurors, gypsies, sybils, hobgoblins, apparitions and the like, are supposed to be under their diabolical government: old Belzebub rules them all. Men will face destructive cannon and mortars, engage each other in the clashing of arms, and meet the horrors of war undaunted, but the devil and his banditti of fiends and emissaries fright them out of their wits, and have a powerful influence in plunging them into superstition, and also in continuing them therein.

This supposed intercourse between mankind and those infernal beings, is by some thought to be miraculous or supernatural ; while others laugh at all the stories of their existence, concluding them to be mere juggle and deception, craftily imposed on the credulous, who are always gaping after something marvellous, miraculous, or supernatural, or after that which they do not understand : and are awkward and unskilful in their examination into nature, or into the truth or reality of things, which is occasioned partly by natural imbecility, and partly by indolence and inattention to nature and reason.

That any magical intercourse or correspondence of mere spirits with mankind, is contradictory to nature, and consequently impossible, has been argued in chapter sixth. And that nothing short of the omnipotent power of God, countermanding his eternal order of nature, and impressing it with new and contrary law, can constitute a miracle has been argued in this, and is an effect surpassing the power of mere creatures, the diabolical nature not excepted. From hence we infer, that devils cannot work miracles. Inattention to reason, and ignorance of the nature of things makes many of mankind give credit to miracles. It seems that by this marvellous way of accounting for things, they think to come off with reputation in their ignorance ; for if nature was nothing but a supernatural whirligig, or an inconstant and irregular piece of mechanism, it would reduce all learning and science to a level with the fanaticism and superstition of the weak and credulous, and put the wise and unwise on a level in point of knowledge, as there would not, on this thesis, be any regular standard in nature, whereby to ascertain the truth and reality of things. What is called sleight-of-hand, is by some people thought to be miraculous. Astrological calculations of nativities, lucky and unlucky days and seasons, are by some regarded, and even moles on the surface of the skin are thought to be portentive of good or bad fortune.

" The Swedish Laplanders, the most ignorant mortals in Europe," are " charged with being conjurors, and are said to have done such feats, by the magic art, as do not at all fall far short of miracles ; that they will give the sailors such winds as they want in any part of their voyage ; that they can inflict and cure diseases at any distance ; and insure people of success in their undertakings ; and yet they are just such poor miserable wretches as used to be charged with witchcraft here," viz : in England and in New England, "and cannot command so much as the necessaries of life : and indeed, none but very credulous and ignorant people give credit to such fables at this day, though the whole world seems to have been bewitched in believing them formerly." "The 24th of March, 1735, an act passed in the Parliament of Great Britain to repeal the statute of I *Jac's*, entitled an act against conjuration, witchcraft, and dealing with evil and wicked spirits, and to repeal an act in Scotland entitled Amentis Witchcraft." It is but forty-six years since the supreme legislature became apprized of the natural impossibility of any magical intercourse between mankind and evil and wicked spirits ; in consequence whereof they repealed their statute laws against it, as they were naturally void, unnecessary, and unworthy of their legislative restriction. For that such a crime had no possible existence in nature, and therefore could not be acted by mankind; though previous to the repeal of those laws, more or less of that island had fallen a sacrifice to them; and the relations of those imaginary criminals were stamped with infamy by such executions, which had the sanction of law, *alias* of the legislature and the judges, and in which many learned attornies have demonstrated the turpitude of such capital offences, and the just sanction of those laws in extirpating such pests of society from the earth; to which the clergy have likewise given their approbation, for that those capital transgressors made too free with their devils.

Furthermore, the repeal of those laws, as far as the wisdom and authority of the British Parliament may be supposed to go, abrogated that command of the law of Moses, which saith, " Thou shalt not suffer a witch to live," and not only so, but the doctrine of the impossibility of intercourse, or of dealing with wicked spirits, forecloses the supposed miraculous casting out of devils, of which we have sundry chronicles in the New Testament.

But to return to the annals of my own country, it will present us with a scene of superstition in the magical way, which will probably equal any that is to be met with in history, to wit: the Salem witchcraft in New England; great numbers of the inhabitants of both sexes were judicially convicted of being wizards and witches, and executed accordingly; some of whom were so infatuated with the delusion, that at their execution they confessed themselves guilty of the sorcery for which they were indicted; nor did the fanaticism meet with a check.

until some of the first families were accused with it, who made such an opposition to the prosecutions, as finally to put an end to any further execution of the Salemites.

Those capital offenders suffered in consequence of certain laws, which, by way of derision, have since been called the *Blue Laws,* in consequence of the multiplicity of superstition, with which they abounded, most of which are repealed ; but those that respect sorcery have had favorite legislators enough to keep them alive and in force to this day.

I recollect an account of prodigies said to have been carried on by the Romish Clergy in France, upon which his most Christian Majesty sent one of his officers to them with the following prohibition, to wit : " by the command of the king, God is forbid to work any more miracles in this place ; " upon which the marvellous work ceased.

There has been so much detection of the artifice, juggle and imposture of the pretenders to miracles, in the world, especially in such parts where learning and science have prevailed, that it should prompt us to be very suspicious of the reality of them, even without entering into any lengthy arguments from the reason and nature of things to evince the utter impossibility of their existence in the creation and providence of God.

We are told, that the first occasion and introduction of miracles into the world, was to prove the divine authority of revelation, and the mission of its first teachers ; be it so.   Upon this plan of evincing the divinity of revelation, it would be necessary that its teachers should always be vested with the power of working miracles ; so that when their authority or the infallibility of the revelation which

they should teach, should at any time be questioned, they
might work a miracle ; or that in such a case God would
do it ; which would end the dispute, provided mankind
were supposed to be judges of miracles, which may be
controverted.   However, admitting that they are possible,
and mankind in the several generations of the world to
be adequate judges of them, and also, that they were
necessary to support the divine mission of the first promulgators of revelation, and the divinity which they
taught ; from the same parity of reasoning, miracles
ought to be continued to the succeeding generations of
mankind, co-extensive with its divine authority, or that
of its teachers.   For why should we in this age of the
world be under obligation to believe the infallibility of
revelation, or the heavenly mission of its teachers, upon
less evidence than those of mankind who lived in the
generations before us ?   For that which may be supposed
to be a rational evidence, and worthy to gain the belief
and assent of mankind at one period of time, must be so
at another ; so that it appears, from the sequel of the
arguments on this subject, that provided miracles were
requisite to establish the divine authority of revelation
originally, it is equally requisite that they be continued
to the latest posterity, to whom the divine legislator may
be supposed to continue such revelation as his law to
mankind.

Nothing is more evident to the understanding part of
mankind, than that in those parts of the world where
learning and science has prevailed, miracles have ceased ;
but in such parts of it as are barbarous and ignorant,
miracles are still in vogue ; which is of itself a strong

presumption that in the infancy of letters, learning and science, or in the world's non-age, those who confided in miracles, as a proof of the divine mission of the first promulgators of revelation, were imposed upon by ficti‑ tious appearances instead of miracles.

Furthermore, the author of Christianity warns us against the impositions of false teachers, and ascribes the signs of the true believers, saying, "And these signs shall follow them that believe, in my name shall they cast out devils, they shall speak with new tongues, they shall take up serpents, and if they drink any deadly thing it shall not hurt them, they shall lay hands on the sick and they shall recover." These are the express words of the founder of Christianity, and are contained in the very commission, which he gave to his eleven Apostles, who were to promulgate his gospel in the world ; so that from their very institution it appears that when the miraculous signs, therein spoken of, failed, they were considered as unbelievers, and consequently no faith or trust to be any longer reposed in them or their successors. For these signs were those which were to perpetuate their mission, and were to be continued as the only evidences of the validity and authenticity of it, and as long as these signs followed, mankind could not be deceived in adhering to the doctrines which the Apostles and their successors taught ; but when these signs failed, their di‑ vine authority ended. Now if any of them will drink a dose of deadly poison, which I could prepare, and it does not " hurt them," I will subscribe to their divine author‑ ity, and end the dispute ; not that I have a disposition to poison any one, nor do I suppose that they would dare to

4

take such a dose as I could prepare for them, which, if
so, would evince that they were unbelievers themselves,
though they are extremely apt to censure others for unbelief, which according to their scheme is a damnable sin.

SECTION IV.

PRAYER CANNOT BE ATTENDED WITH MIRACULOUS CONSEQUENCES.

PRAYER to God is no part of a rational religion, nor
did reason ever dictate it, but, was it duly attended to,
it would teach us the contrary.

To make known our wants to God by prayer, or to
communicate any intelligence concerning ourselves or
the universe to him, is impossible, since his omniscient
mind has a perfect knowledge of all things, and therefore is beholden to none of our correspondence to inform
himself of our circumstances, or of what would be
wisest and best to do for us in all possible conditions
and modes of existence, in our never ending duration of
being   These, with the infinitude of things, have been
eternally deliberated by the omniscient mind, who can
admit of no additional intelligence, whether by prayer
or otherwise, which renders it nugatory.

We ought to act up to the dignity of our nature, and
demean ourselves, as creatures of our rank and capacity,
and not presume to dictate any thing, less or more, to
the governor of the universe ; who rules not by our
proscriptions, but by eternal and infinite reason. To
pray to God, or to make supplication to him, requesting

certain favors for ourselves, or from any, or all the species, is inconsistent with the relation which subsists between God and man. Whoever has a just sense of the absolute perfection of God, and of their own imperfection, and natural subjection to his providence, cannot but from thence infer the impropriety of praying or supplicating to God, for this, that, or the other thing; or of remonstrating against his providence: inasmuch, as " known to God are all our wants; " and as we know, that we ourselves are inadequate judges of what would be best for us, all things considered. God looks through the immensity of things, and understands the harmony, moral beauty and decorum of the whole, and will by no means change his purposes, or alter the nature of the things themselves for any of our entreaties or threats. To pray, entreat, or make supplication to God, is neither more nor less than dictating to eternal reason, and entering into the province and prerogative of the Almighty; if this is not the meaning and import of prayer, it has none at all, that extends to the final events and consequences of things. To pray to God with a sense, that the prayer we are making will not be granted any more for our making it, or that our prayer will make no alteration in the state, order or disposal of things at all, or that the requests, which we make, will be no more likely to be granted, or the things themselves conferred upon us by God, than as though we had not prayed for them, would be stupidity or outright mockery, or " to be seen of men," in order to procure from them some temporary advantages. But on the other hand for us to suppose, that our prayers or praises do in any one instance or more alter the eternal constitution of things, or of the providence of God, is the same as to suppose ourselves so far forth to hold a share in the divine government, for our prayers must be supposed to effect something or nothing, if they effect nothing they are good for nothing; but that they should effect any alteration in the nature of things, or providence of God, is inadmissible : for if they did, we should interfere with the providence of God in a certain degree, by arrogating it to ourselves. For if there are any particulars in providence, which God does not govern by his order of nature, they do not belong to the providence of God, but of man ; for if in any instance, God is moved by the prayers, entreaties, or supplications of his creatures, to alter his providence, or to do that in conformity thereto, which otherwise, in the course of his providence, he would not have done ; then it would necessarily follow, that as far as such alteration may be supposed to take place, God does not govern by eternal and infinite reason, but on the contrary is governed himself by the prayer of man.

Our great proficients in prayer must need think themselves to be of great importance in the scale of being, otherwise they would not indulge themselves in the notion, that the God of nature would subvert his laws, or bend his providence in conformity to their prayers. But it may be objected, that they pray conditionally, to wit: that God would answer their prayers, provided they are agreeable to his providential order or disposal of things; but to consider prayer in such a sense renders it, not only useless, but impertinent ; for the laws of nature would produce their natural effects as well without it, as with it. The sum total of such conditional prayer could amount to no more than this, viz : that God would not regard them at all, but that he would conduct the kingdom of his providence agreeable to the absolute perfections of his nature ; and who in the exercise of common sense would imagine that God would do otherwise ?

The nature of the immense universality of things having been eternally adjusted, constituted and settled, by the profound thought, perfect wisdom, impartial justice, immense goodness, and omnipotent power of God, it is the greatest arrogance in us to attempt an alteration thereof. If we demean ourselves worthy of a rational happiness, the laws of the moral system, already established, will afford it to us ; and as to physical evils, prudent economy may make them tolerable, or ward most of them off for a season, though they will unavoidably bring about the separation of a soul and body, and terminate with animal life, whether we pray for or against it.

To pray for any thing, which we can obtain by the due application of our natural powers, and neglect the means of procuring it, is impertinence and laziness in the abstract ; and to pray for that which God in the course of his providence, has put out of our power to obtain, is only murmuring against God, and finding fault with his providence, or acting the inconsiderate part of a child ; *for example,* to pray for more wisdom, understanding, grace or faith ; for a more robust constitution — handsomer figure, or more of a gigantic size, would be the same as telling God, that we are dissatisfied

with our inferiority in the order of being ; that neither
our souls nor bodies suit us ; that he has been too sparing
of his beneficence ; that we want more wisdom, and organs better fitted for show, agility and superiority.   But
we ought to consider, that " *we cannot add one cubit to
our stature,*" or alter the construction of our organic
frame ; and that our mental talents are finite ; and that
in a vast variety of proportions and disproportions, as
our Heavenly Father in his order of nature, and scale of
being saw fit ; who has nevertheless for the encourage-
ment of intelligent nature ordained, that it shall be capable of improvement, and consequently of enlargement ;
therefore, " *whosoever lacketh wisdom,*" instead of " *ask-
ing it of God,*" let him improve what he has, that he
may enlarge the original stock ; this is all the possible
way of gaining in wisdom and knowledge, a competency
of which will regulate our faith.   But it is too common
for great faith and little knowledge to unite in the same
person ; such persons are beyond the reach of argument
and their faith immovable, though it cannot remove
mountains.   The only way to procure food, raiment, or
the necessaries or conveniences of life, is by natural
means ; we do not get them by wishing or praying for,
but by actual exertion ; and the only way to obtain virtue or morality is to practice and habituate ourselves to
it, and not to pray to God for it : he has naturally furnished us with talents or faculties suitable for the exercise and enjoyment of religion, and it is our business to
improve them aright, or we must suffer the consequences
of it.   We should conform ourselves to reason, the path
of moral rectitude, and in so doing, we cannot fail of

recommending ourselves to God, and to our own consciences. This is all the religion which reason knows
or can ever approve of.

Moses, the celebrated prophet and legislator of the
Israelites, ingratiated himself into their esteem, by the
stratagem of prayer, and pretended intimacy with God;
he acquaints us, that he was once admitted to a sight of
his BACK-PARTS! and that *" no man can see "* his *" face
and live; "* and at other times we are told that he
*" talked with God, face to face, as a man talketh with
his friend; "* and also that at times God waxed wroth
with Israel, and how Moses prayed for them; and at
other times, that he ordered Aaron to offer sweet incense
to God, which *appeased his wrath,* and prevented his
destroying Israel in his *hot displeasure!* These are the
footsteps, by which we may trace sacerdotal dominion to
its source, and explore its progress in the world. *"And
the Lord said unto Moses, how long will this people pro-
voke me? I will smite them with the pestilence, and
disinherit them, and I will make of thee a great nation,
and mightier than they,"* but Moses advertises God of
the injury, which so rash a procedure would do to his
character among the nations; and also reminds him of
his promise to Israel, saying, *"Now if thou shall kill all
this people as one man, then the nations, which have
heard the fame of thee will speak, saying, because the
Lord was not able to bring this people into the land,
which he swear unto them, therefore he hath slain them
in the wilderness."* That Moses should thus advise the
omniscient God, of dishonorable consequences which
would attend a breach of promise, which he tells us,

that God was unadvisedly about to make with the tribes
of Israel, had not his remonstrance prevented it, is very
extraordinary and repugnant to reason ; yet to an eye of
faith it would exalt the man Moses, " and make him
very great ; " for if we may credit his history of the
matter, he not only averted God's judgment against Israel,
and prevented them from being cut off as a nation, but
by the same prayer procured for them a pardon of their
sin.   " *Pardon, I beseech thee, the iniquity of this people,*" and in the next verse follows the answer, " *and
the Lord said I have pardoned according to thy word.*"
It seems that God had the power, but Moses had the
dictation of it, and saved Israel from the wrath and
pestilential fury of a jealous God ; and that he procured
them a pardon of their sin, " *for the Lord thy God is
a jealous God.*"   Jealousy can have no existence in that
mind, which possesses perfect knowledge, and consequently cannot, without the greatest impropriety, be
ascribed to God, who knows all things, and needed none
of the admonitions, advice or intelligence of Moses, or
any of his dictatorial prayers.   "*And the Lord hearkened unto me at that time also ;* " intimating that it was
a common thing for him to do the like.   When teachers
can once make the people believe that God answers their
prayers, and that their eternal interest is dependent on
them, they soon raise themselves to opulency, rule and
high sounding titles ; as that of *His Holiness — the
Reverend Father in God — The Holy Poker — Bishop
of Souls* — and a variety of other such like appellations,
derogatory to the honor or just prerogative of God ; as
is Joshua's history concerning the Lord's hearkening

unto him at the battle of the Amorites, wherein he informs us, that he ordered the sun to stand still, saying, *"Sun stand thou still upon Giboen, and thou Moon in the valley of Ajalon, so the Sun stood still and the Moon stayed until the people had avenged themselves upon their enemies;"* so the Sun stood still in the midst of Heaven, and hasted not to go down about a whole day;"* and then adds, by way of supremacy to himself above all others, and in direct contradiction to the before recited passages of Moses concerning the Lord's hearkening unto him, or to any other man but himself, saying, *"And there was no day like that before it, or after it, that the Lord hearkened unto the voice of a man."* There is not any thing more evident than that if the representation given by Joshua, as matter of fact, is true, those exhibited by Moses concerning the Lord's hearkening unto him are not: though the representations of fact by Moses and by Joshua, are allowed to be both canonical, yet it is impossible that both can be true. However, astronomy being but little understood in the age in which Joshua lived, and the earth being in his days thought to be at rest, and the sun to revolve round it, makes it in no way strange, that he caught himself by ordering the sun to stand still, which having since been discovered to have been the original fixed position of that luminous body, eclipses the miraculous interposition of Joshua. Furthermore, if we but reflect that on that very day Israel vanquished the Amorites with a great slaughter, *" and chased them along the way that goeth to Bethoron, and smote them to Azekah, and unto Makkedah,"* in so great a hurry of war, clashing of arms, exasperation and eleva-

4 *

tion of mind, in consequence of such triumphant victory, they could make but a partial observation on the length of the day ; and being greatly elated with such an extraordinary day's work, Joshua took the advantage of it, and told them that it was an uncommon day for duration ; that he had interposed in the system and prescribed to the sun to stand still about a whole day ; and that they had two days' time to accomplish those great feats. The belief of such a miraculous event to have taken place in the solar system, in consequence of the influence which Joshua insinuated that he had with God, would most effectually establish his authority among the people ; for if God would hearken to his voice well might man. This is the cause why the bulk of mankind in all ages and countries of the world, have been so much infatuated by their ghostly teachers, whom they have ever imagined to have had a special influence with God Almighty.

CHAPTER VII.

SECTION I.

THE VAGUENESS AND UNINTELLIGIBLENESS OF THE PROPHECIES, RENDER THEM INCAPABLE OF PROVING REVELATION.

PROPHECY is by some thought to be miraculous, and by others to be supernatural, and there are others, who indulge themselves in an opinion, that they amount to no more than mere political conjectures. Some nations have feigned an intercourse with good spirits by the art of divination ; and others with evil ones by the art of magic ;

and most nations have pretended to an intercourse with the world of spirits both ways.

The Romans trusted much to their sibylline oracles and soothsayers; the Babylonians to their magicians and astrologers; the Egyptians and Persians to their magicians; and the Jews to their seers or prophets; and all nations and individuals, discover an anxiety for an intercourse with the world of spirits; which lays a foundation for artful and designing men, to impose upon them. But if the foregoing arguments in chapter sixth, respecting the natural impossibility of an intercourse of any unbodied or imperceptible mental beings with mankind, are true, then the foretelling of future events can amount to nothing more than political illusion. For prophecy as well as all other sorts of prognostication must be supernaturally inspired, or it could be no more than judging of future events from mere probability or guess-work, as the astronomers ingenuously confess in their calculations, by saying: "Judgment of the weather," &c. So also respecting astrology, provided there is any such thing as futurity to be learned from it, it would be altogether a natural discovery; for neither astronomy nor astrology claim anything of a miraculous or supernatural kind, but their calculations are meant to be predicated on the order and course of nature, with which our senses are conversant, and with which inspiration or the mere co-operation of spirits is not intended to act as part. So also concerning prophecy, if it be considered to be merely natural, (we will not at present dispute whether it is true or false) upon this position it stands on the footing of probability or mere conjecture and uncertainty. But as to the doctrine of any supernatural agency of the divine mind on ours, which is commonly called inspiration, it has been sufficiently confuted in chapter sixth; which arguments need not be repeated, nor does it concern my system to settle the question, whether prophecy should be denominated miraculous or supernatural, inasmuch as both these doctrines have been confuted; though it is my opinion, that were we to trace the notion of supernatural to its source, it would finally terminate in that which is denominated miraculous; for that which is above or beyond nature, if it has any positive existence, must be miraculous.

The writings of the prophets are most generally so loose, vague and indeterminate in their meaning, or in the grammar of their present translation, that the prophecies will as well answer to events in one period of time, as in another; and are equally applicable to a variety of events, which have and are still taking place in the world, and are liable to so many different interpretations, that they are incapable of being understood or explained, except upon arbitrary principles, and therefore cannot be admitted as a proof of revelation; *as for instance, " it shall come to pass in the last days, saith God."* Who can understand the accomplishment of the prophecies, that are expressed. after this sort? for every day in its turn has been, and will in its succession be the last day; and if we advert to the express words of the prophecy, *to wit, " the last days,"* there will be an uncertain plurality *" of last days,"* which must be understood to be short of a month, or a year; or it should have been expressed thus, and it shall come to pass in the last months or years, instead of days : and if it had mentioned last years, it would be a just construction to suppose, that it included a less number of years than a century ; but as the prophecy mentions *" last days,"* we are at a loss, which among the plurality of them to assign for the fulfilling of the prophecy.

Furthermore, we cannot learn from the prophecy, in what month, year, or any other part of duration those last days belong ; so that we can never tell when such vague prophecies are to take place, they therefore remain the arbitrary prerogative of fanatics to prescribe their events in any age or period of time, when their distempered fancies may think most eligible : there are other prophecies still more abstruse ; *to wit, "And one said unto the man clothed in linen, which was upon the waters of the river, how long shall it be to the end of these wonders? and I heard the man clothed in linen, which was upon the waters of the river, when he held up his right hand and his left hand unto Heaven, and sware by him that liveth forever, that it should be for an time, times and an half."* The question in the prophecy is asked *" how long shall it be to the end of these wonders? "* and the answer is given with the solemnity of an oath, *" it shall be for a time, times and a half."* A *time* is an indefinite part of duration, and so are *times,* and the third description of time is as indefinite as either of the former descriptions of it ; *to wit, " and an half; "* that is to say, *half a time.* There is no certain term given in any or either of the three descriptions of the end of the wonders alluded to, whereby any or all of them together are capable of computation, as there is no

certain period marked out to begin or end a calculation.
To compute an indefinite *time* in the single number or
quantity of duration is impossible, and to compute an
uncertain plurality of such indefinite *times* is equally
perplexing and impracticable ; and lastly, to define *half
a time* by any possible succession of its parts, is a contradiction, for *half a time* includes no time at all ; inasmuch as the smallest conception or possible moment or
criterion of duration, is *a time*, or otherwise, by the
addition of ever so many of those parts together, they
would not prolong a period ; so that there is not, and
cannot be such a part of time, as *half a time*, for be it
supposed to be ever so momentous, yet if includes any
part of duration, it is *a time*, and not *half a time*.   Had
the prophet said half a year, half a day, or half a minute, he would have spoken intelligibly ; but *half a time*
has no existence at all, and consequently no period could
ever possibly arrive in the succession or order of time,
when there could be an end to the wonders alluded to ;
and in this sense only, the prophecy is intelligible ; to
wit, that it will never come to pass.

The revelation of St. John the divine, involves the
subject of time, if possible, in still greater inconsistencies,
viz : *"And to the woman was given two wings of a great
eagle, that she might fly into the wilderness, into her
place : Where she is nourished for a time, and times and
half a time."* *"And the angel which I saw stand upon
the sea and upon the earth lifted up his hands to heaven,
and sware by him that liveth forever and ever, who created heaven and the things that therein are, and the earth
and the things that therein are, and the sea and the*

things which are therein, that there should be time no longer." Had this tremendous oath been verified there could have been no farther disputations on the calculation of "*time and times and half a time,*" (or about any thing else) for its succession would have reached its last and final period at that important crisis when time should have been "no longer." The solar system must have ceased its motions, from which we compute the succession of time, and the race of man would have been extinct; for as long as they may be supposed to exist, time must of necessary consequence have existed also; and since the course of nature, including the generations of mankind, has been continued from the time of the positive denunciation of the angel to this day, we may safely conclude, that his interference in the system of nature, was perfectly romantic.

The apostle Peter, at the first Christian pentecost, objecting to the accusation of their being drunk with new wine, explains the prophecy of the prophet Joel, who prophesied of the events which were to take place in the last days, as coming to pass at that early period; his words are handed down to us as follows: "*But this is that which is spoken by the prophet Joel, and it shall come to pass in the last days, saith God, that I will pour out my spirit upon all flesh, and your sons and your daughters shall prophecy, and your young men shall see visions, and your old men shall dream dreams.*"

The history of the out-pouring of the spirit at the Pentecost, admitting it to have been a fact, would have been very inadequate to the prophetical prediction, *viz:* *I will pour out my spirit upon all flesh;* the most favorable construction is that the prophet meant human flesh, *i. e.*, all human flesh ; but instead of a universal effusion of the spirit, it appears to have been restricted to a select number, who were collected together at Jerusalem, and the concourse of spectators thought them to be delirious. It may however be supposed, that St. Peter was a better judge of the accomplishment of the prophecy than I am : well then, admitting his application of the prophecy of the last days to take place at the first pentecost ; it being now more than seventeen hundred years ago, they consequently could not have been the last days.

Still a query arises, whether every of the prophecies, which were predicted to be fulfilled in the last days, must not have been accomplished at that time ; or whether any of the prophecies thus expressed are still to be completed by any events which may in future take place ; or by any which have taken place since those last days called pentecost ; or whether any prophecy whatever can be fulfilled more than once ; and if so, how many times ; or how is it possible for us, out of the vast variety of events (in which there is so great a similarity) which one in particular to ascribe to its right prediction among the numerous prophecies ?

Furthermore, provided some of the prophecies should point out some particular events, which have since taken place, there might have been previous grounds of probability, that such or such events would in the ordinary course of things come to pass ; *for instance,* it is no ways extraordinary, that the prophet Jeremiah should be able to predict that Nebuchadnezzar, king of Babylon, should take Jerusalem, when we consider the power of the Babylonish empire at that time, and the feebleness of the Jews. *"The word, which came to Jeremiah from the Lord, when Nebuchadnezzar king of Babylon and all his army, and all the kingdoms of the earth of his dominion, and all the people fought against Jerusalem, and against all the cities thereof, saying, thus saith the Lord the God of Israel, go and speak unto Zedekiah king of Judah, and tell him thus saith the Lord, behold, I will give this city of Jerusalem into the hand of the king of Babylon."* No politicians could at the time of the prediction be much at a loss respecting the fate of Jerusalem. Nor would it be at all evidential to any candid and ingenious enquirer, that God had any manner of agency in fabricating the prophecies, though some of them should seem to decypher future events, as they might, to human appearance, turn out right, merely from accident or contingency. It is very improbable, or rather incompatible with human nature, that the prophecy of Micah will ever come to pass, who predicts that *" they,"* speaking of mankind, *" shall beat their swords into plough-shares, and their spears into pruning-hooks ; nation shall not lift up sword against nation, neither shall they learn war any more."* Some of the prophecies are so apparently contradictory, that they contain their own confutation ; as for instance, the prophecy of Micaiah contained in the book of Chronicles, which probably is as absurd as any thing that is to be met with in story : *"* And when he was come unto the king, the king said unto him, Micaiah, shall we go to Ramoth Gilead to battle, or shall I forbear ? and he said go ye up and prosper, and they shall be delivered into your hand, and the king said unto him, how many times shall I adjure thee, that thou shalt tell me nothing, but that which is true in the name of the Lord? then he said I did see all Israel scattered upon the mountains, as sheep that have no shepherd, and the Lord said, these have no master, let them return, therefore, every man to his house in peace: and the king said unto Jehoshaphat, did not I tell thee, that he would prophecy no good concerning me, but evil?" "Again he said, therefore, hear the word of the Lord — I saw the Lord sitting upon his throne, and all the host of Heaven standing on his right hand and on his left, and the Lord said who shall entice Ahab, King of Israel, that he may go up and fall at Ramoth Gilead, and one spake saying after this manner, and another saying after that manner; then there came out a spirit and stood before the Lord, and said I will entice him, and the Lord said unto him wherewith? And he said I will go forth and be a lying spirit in the mouth of all his prophets, and the Lord said thou shalt entice him and thou shalt prevail; go out and do even so. Now therefore, behold the Lord hath put a lying spirit in the mouth of these thy prophets and the Lord hath spoken evil against thee." It is observable that the prophet at first predicted the prosperity of Ahab, saying, "go ye up and prosper, and they shall be delivered into your hand," but after a little adjurement by the king, he alters his prediction and prophecies diametrically the reverse. What is more certain than that the event of the expedition against Ramoth Gilead must have comported with the one or the other of his prophecies? Certain it was, that Ahab would take it or not take it, he must either prosper or not prosper, as there would be no third way or means between these two; and it appears that the prophet was determined to be in the right of it by his prophecy both ways. It further appears from his prophecy, that there was a great consultation in Heaven to entice Ahab King of Israel to his destruction, and that a certain lying spirit came and stood before the Lord, and proposed to him to go out and be a lying spirit in the mouth of the king's prophets. But what is the most incredible is, that God should countenance it, and give him positive orders to falsify the truth to the other prophets. It appears that Micaiah in his first prophecy, viz: "Go up to Ramoth Gilead and prosper, and they shall be delivered into your hand," acted in concert with the lying spirit which stood before the Lord, but afterwards acted the treacherous part by prophecying the truth, which, if we may credit his account, was in direct opposition to the scheme of Heaven.

SECTION II.

THE CONTENTIONS WHICH SUBSISTED BETWEEN THE PROPH-
ETS RESPECTING THEIR VERACITY, AND THEIR INCON-
SISTENCIES WITH ONE ANOTHER, AND WITH THE NATURE
OF THINGS, AND THEIR OMISSION IN TEACHING THE
DOCTRINE OF IMMORTALITY, PRECLUDES THE DIVINITY
OF THEIR PROPHECIES.

WHOEVER examines the writings of the prophets will discover a spirit of strife and contention among them; they would charge each other with fallacy and deception; disputations of this kind are plentifully interspersed through the writings of the prophets; we

will transcribe a few of those passages out of many:
" Thus saith the Lord to the foolish prophets that follow their own spirit, and have found nothing, they have
seen vanity and lying divination, saying the Lord saith,
and the Lord hath not sent them, and they have made
others to hope that they would confirm the word." And
in another place, " I have not sent these prophets, yet
they ran ; I have not spoken unto them, yet they prophecy." Again, " I have heard what the prophets said,
that prophecy lies in my name, saying, I have dreamed,
I have dreamed, yet they are the prophets of the deceit
of their own hearts." And again, " Yea, they are
greedy dogs, which can never have enough, and they
are shepherds that cannot understand ; they all look to
their own way, every one for his gain from his quarter."

It being the case that there was such a strife among
the prophets to recommend themselves to the people,
and every art and dissimulation having been practised by
them to gain power and superiority, all which artifice
was to be judged of by the great vulgar, or in some instances by the political views of the Jewish Sanhedrim,
how could those who were cotemporaries with the several
prophets, distinguish the premised true prophets from
the false ? Much less, how can we, who live more than
seventeen hundred years since the last of them, be able
to distinguish them apart ? And yet, without the knowledge of this distinction, we cannot with propriety give
credit to any of them, even admitting there were some
true prophets among them. Nor is it possible for us to
know but that their very institution was merely a reach
of policy of the Israelitish and Judaic governments, the

more easily, implicitly and effectually to keep their people in subordination, by inculcating a belief that they were ruled with special directions from heaven, which in fact originated from the Sanhedrim. Many other nations have made use of much the same kind of policy.

In the 22d chapter of Genesis, we have a history of a very extraordinary command from God to Abraham, and of a very unnatural attempt of his to obey it. "And it came to pass after these things that God did tempt Abraham, and he said unto him, Abraham, and he said behold here I am, and he said take now thy son Isaac, whom thou lovest, and get thee to the land of Moriah, and offer him there for a burnt offering upon one of the mountains which I will tell thee of;" "And they came to the place which God had told him of, and Abraham built an altar there, and laid the wood in order, and bound Isaac his son, and laid him on the altar upon the wood; and Abraham stretched forth his hand and took the knife to slay his son." Shocking attempt! Murder is allowed by mankind in general to be the most capital crime that is possible to be acted among men; it would therefore be incompatible with the divine nature to have enjoined it by a positive command to Abraham to have killed his son; a murder of all others the most unnatural and cruel and attended with the most aggravating circumstances, not merely from a prescribed breach of the ties of parental affection, but from the consideration that the child was to be (if we may credit the command,) offered to God as a religious sacrifice. What could have been a more complicated wickedness than the obedience of this command would have been? and what

can be more absurd than to suppose that it came from
God? It is argued, in vindication of the injunction to
Abraham to kill his son, that it was merely for a trial of
his obedience, and that God never designed to have him
do it; to prevent which an angel from heaven called to
him and gave him counter orders, not to slay his son;
but to suppose that God needed such an experiment, or
any other, in order to know whether Abraham would be
obedient to his commands, is utterly incompatible with
his omniscience, who without public exhibitions understands all things; so that had the injunction been in
itself, fit and reasonable, and also from God, the com-
pliance or non-compliance of Abraham thereto, could
not have communicated any new idea to the divine mind.
Every part of the conduct of mankind is a trial of their
obedience and is known to God, as well as the particular
conduct of Abraham; besides in the canonical writings,
we read that *"God cannot be tempted with evil, neither
tempteth he any man."* How then can it be, *" that God
did tempt Abraham?"* a sort of employment which, in
scripture, is commonly ascribed to the devil. It is a
very common thing to hear Abraham extolled for at-
tempting to comply with the supposed command of sac-
rificing his son; but it appears to me, that it had been
wiser and more becoming the character of a virtuous
man, for Abraham to have replied in answer to the injunction as follows, to wit, that it could not possibly have come from God; who was the fountain of
goodness and perfection, and unchangeable in his nature,
who had endowed him with reason and understanding,
whereby he knew his duty to God, his son, and to him-

self, better than to kill his only son, and offer him as a religious sacrifice to God, for God would never have implanted in his mind such a strong affection towards him, nor such a conscious sense of duty to provide for, protect and succor him in all duties, and to promote his happiness and well being, provided he had designed that he should have laid violent hands on his life. And inasmuch as the command was, in itself, morally speaking, unfit, and altogether unworthy of God, he presumed that it never originated from him, but from some inhuman, cruel and destructive being, who delighted in wo, and pungent grief; for God could not have been the author of so base an injunction, nor could he be pleased with so inhuman and sinful a sacrifice.

Moses in his last chapter of Deuteronomy crowns his history with the particular account of his own death and burial. "So Moses, the servant of the Lord, died there, in the land of Moab, according to the word of the Lord, and he buried him in a valley, in the land of Moab, over against Bethpeor, but no man knew of his sepulchre unto this day ; and Moses was an hundred and twenty years old when he died, his eyes were not dim, nor his natural force abated, and the children of Israel wept for Moses in the plains of Moab thirty days." This is the only historian in the circle of my reading, who has ever given the public a particular account of his own death, and how old he was at that decisive period, where he died, who buried him, and where he was buried, and withal of the number of days his friends and acquaintances mourned and wept for him. I must confess I do not expect to be able to advise the

public of the term of my life, nor the circumstances of
my death and burial, nor of the days of the weeping or
laughing of my survivors.

Part of the laws of Moses were arbitrary impositions
upon the tribes of Israel, and have no foundation in the
reason and fitness of things, particularly that in which
he inculcates punishing the children for the iniquities of
the father ; "visiting the iniquities of the fathers upon
the children, and upon the children's children unto the
third and fourth generation." There is no reason to be
given, why the iniquity of the father might not as well
have involved the fifth, sixth and seventh generations,
and so on to the latest posterity in guilt and punishment,
as the first four generations ; for if it was possible, that
the iniquity of the father could be justly visited upon
any of his posterity, who were not accomplices with him
in the iniquity, or were not some way or other aiding
or accessary in it, then the iniquity might as justly be
visited upon any one of the succeeding generations as
upon another, or upon the generation of any indifferent
person : for arbitrary imputations of iniquity are equally
absurd in all supposable cases ; so that if we once admit
the possibility of visiting iniquity upon any others than
the perpetrators, be they who they will, we overturn our
natural and scientifical notions of a personal retribution
of justice among mankind. It is, in plain English,
punishing the innocent for the sin of the guilty. But
virtue or vice cannot be thus visited or imputed from the
fathers to the unoffending children, or to children's
children ; or which is the same thing, from the guilty to
the innocent ; for moral good or evil is mental and per-

sonal, which cannot be transferred, changed or altered
from one person to another, but is inherently connected
with its respective personal actors, and constitutes a
quality or habit, and is the merit or demerit of the respective agents or proficients in moral good or evil, and
is by nature inalienable, "The righteousness of the
righteous shall be upon him, and the wickedness of the
wicked shall be upon him." But as we shall have occasion to argue this matter at large in the twelfth chapter
of this treatise, where we shall treat of the imputed sin
of Adam to his posterity, and of imputative righteousness, we will discuss the subject of imputation no farther
in this place. However, the unjust practice of punishing the children for the iniquity of the father having
been an ordinance of Moses, was more or less continued
by the Israelites, as in the case of Achan and his children. "And Joshua and all Israel with him took
Achan the son of Zorah, and the silver and the garment,
and the wedge of gold, and his sons, and his daughters,
and his oxen, and his asses, and his sheep, and his tent,
and all that he had, and brought them to the valley of
Achor, and all Israel stoned him with stones, and burned
them with fire, after they had stoned them with stones,
and they raised over him a great heap of stones unto
this day; so the Lord turned from the fierceness of his
anger." "*Fierce anger*" is incompatible with the divine perfection, nor is the cruel extirpation of the innocent family, and live stock of Achan, to be accounted for
on principles of reason. This flagrant injustice of punishing the children for the iniquity of the father had
introduced a proverb in Israel, viz: "The fathers have

eaten sour grapes and the children's teeth are set on edge." But the prophet Ezekiel in the 18th chapter of his prophecies, has confuted Moses's statutes of visiting. the iniquities of the father upon the children, and repealed them with the authority of *thus saith the Lord,* which was the manner of expression by which they were promulgated. But the prophet Ezekiel did not repeal those statutes of Moses merely by the authority of *thus saith the Lord,* but over and above gives the reason for it, otherwise he could not have repealed them; for Moses enacted them as he relates, from as high authority as Ezekiel could pretend to in nullifying them; so that had he not produced reason and argument, it would have been " thus saith the Lord," against " thus saith the Lord." But Ezekiel reasons conclusively, viz : " The word of the Lord came unto me again, saying, what meat ye that ye use this proverb concerning the land of Israel, saying, the fathers have eaten sour grapes and the children's teeth are set on edge; as I live, saith the Lord God, ye shall not have occasion any more to use this proverb in Israel. Behold all souls are mine, as the soul of the father so also the soul of the son is mine; the soul that sinneth it shall die, the son shall not bear the iniquity of the father, neither shall the father bear the iniquity of the son, the righteousness of the righteous shall be upon him, and the wickedness of the wicked shall be upon him, therefore, I will judge you, O house of Israel, every one according to their ways saith the Lord God." It is observable, that the prophet ingeniously says, " Ye shall not have occasion any more to use this proverb in Israel," implicitly acknowledging that the law of Moses had given occasion to that proverb, nor was it possible to remove that proverb or grievance to which the Israelites were liable on account of visiting the iniquities of the fathers upon the children, but by the repeal of the statute of Moses in that case made and provided; which was effectually done by Ezekiel: in consequence whereof the administration of justice became disencumbered of the embarrassments under which it had labored for many centuries. Thus it appears, that those laws, denominated the laws of God, are not infallible, but have their exceptions and may be dispensed with.

Under the dispensation of the law a breach of the Sabbath was a capital offence. "And while the children of Israel were in the wilderness, they found a man that gathered sticks on the Sabbath day, and the Lord said unto Moses, the man shall surely be put to death, and all the congregation shall stone him with stones without the camp; and all the congregation brought him without the camp and stoned him with stones, and he died, as the Lord commanded Moses." The very institution of the Sabbath was in itself arbitrary, otherwise it would not have been changed from the last to the first day of the week. For those ordinances which are predicated on the reason and fitness of things can never change : as that which is once morally fit, always remains so, and is immutable, nor could the same crime, in justice, deserve death in Moses's time (as in the instance of the Israelite's gathering sticks), and but a pecuniary fine in ours; as in the instance of the breach of Sabbath in these times.

Furthermore, the order of nature respecting day and night, or the succession of time, is such, as renders it impossible that any identical part of time, which constitutes one day, can do it to all the inhabitants of the globe at the same time, or in the same period. Day is perpetually dawning, and night commencing to some or other of the inhabitants of the terraqueous ball without intermission. At the distance of fifteen degrees of longitude to the east of us, the day begins an hour sooner than it does with us here in Vermont, and with us an hour sooner than it does fifteen degrees to the westward, and thus it continues in succession round the globe, and night as regularly revolving after it, succeeding each other in their alternate rounds ; so that when it is mid-day with us, it is mid-night with our species, denominated the *Periæci*, who live under the same parallel of latitude with us, but under a directly opposite meridian ; so likewise, when it is mid-day with them, it is mid-night with us. Thus it appears that the same identical part of time, which composes our days, compose their nights, and while we are keeping Sunday, they are in their midnight dreams ; nor is it possible in nature, that the same identical part of time, which makes the first day of the week wh us, should make the first day of the week with the inhabitants on the opposite side of the globe. The apostle James speaks candidly on this subject, saying, " Some esteem one day above another, others esteem every day alike, let every one be fully persuaded in his own mind," and keep the laws of the land. It was unfortunate for the Israelite who was accused of gathering sticks on the Israelitish Sabbath, that he was convicted of it; for though by the law of his people he must have died, yet the act for which he suffered was no breach of the law of nature. Supposing that very delinquent should come to this world again, and gather sticks on Saturday in this country, he might as an hireling receive his wages for it, without being exposed to a similar prosecution of that of Moses; and provided he should gather sticks on our Sunday, his wages would atone for his crime instead of his life, since modern legislators have abated the rigor of the law for which he died.

The barbarous zeal of the prophet Samuel in hewing Agag to pieces after he was made prisoner by Saul, king of Israel, could not proceed from a good spirit, nor would such cruelty be permitted towards a prisoner in any civilized nation at this day. " And Samuel hewed Agag to pieces before the Lord in Gilgal." The unmanly deed seems to be mentioned with a phiz of religion, viz: that it was done before the Lord; but that cannot alter the nature of the act itself, for every act of mankind, whether good or evil, is done before the Lord, as much as Samuel's hewing Agag to pieces. The orders which Samuel gave unto Saul, (as he says by the word of the Lord) to cut off the posterity of the Amalekites, and to destroy them utterly, together with the cause of God's displeasure with them, are unworthy of God as may be seen at large in the 15th chapter of the Book of Samuel. " Spare them not, but slay both man and woman, infant and suckling, ox and sheep, camel and ass." The ostensible reason for all this, was, because the ancestors of the Amalekites, as long before the days of Samuel as when the children of Israel came out of Egypt, which was near five hundred

years, had ambushed and fought against Israel, in their
passage from thence to the land which they afterwards
inhabited.   Although it appears from the history of Moses
and Joshua, that Israel was going to disposess them of
their country, which is thought to be a sufficient cause of
war in these days.   It is true they insinuaté that the
Lord had given the land to the children of Israel, yet
it appears that they had to fight for it and get it by the
hardest, notwithstanding, as is the case with nations in
these days, and ever has been since the knowledge of
history.

But be the old quarrel between Israel and Amalek as it
will, it cannot on any principle be supposed, the successors of those Amalekites, in the days of Samuel, could
be guilty of any premised transgressions of their prede-
cessors.   The sanguinary laws of Moses did not admit of
visiting the iniquities of the fathers upon the children in
the line of succession, farther than to the fourth generation, but the Amalekites against whom Samuel had
denounced the wrath of God, by the hand of Saul, were
at a much greater remove from those their progenitors,
who were charged with the crime for which they were
cut off as a nation.   Nor is it compatible with reason to
suppose, that God ever directed either Moses or Joshua
to extirpate the Canaanitish nations.   " And we took all
his cities at that time, and utterly destroyed the men and
the women, and the little ones of every city, we left none
to remain."   There is not more propriety in ascribing
these cruelties to God, than those that were perpetrated
by the Spaniards against the Mexican and Peruvian
Indians or natives of America.   Every one who dares to

exercise his reason, free from bias, will readily discern, that the inhumanities exercised towards the Canaanites and Amorites, Mexicans and Peruvians, were detestably wicked, and could not be approbated by God, or by rational and good men. Undoubtedly avarice and domination were the causes of those abounding cruelties, in which religion had as little to do as in the crusades of the holy land (so called.)

The writings of the prophets abound with prodigies, strange and unnatural events. The walls of Jericho are represented to have fallen to the ground in consequence of a blast of ram's horns; Balaam's ass to speak to his master, and the prophet Elijah is said to have been carried off bodily into heaven by a chariot, in a whirlwind. Strange stories! But other scriptures tell us, "Flesh and blood cannot inherit the kingdom of God." The history of the affront, which the little children of Bethel gave the prophet Elisha, his cursing them, and their destruction by the bears, has the appearance of a fable. That Elisha should be so exasperated at the children for calling him *bald head,* and telling him *to go up,* was rather a sample of ill breeding; most gentlemen would have laughed at the joke, instead of cursing them, or being instrumental in their destruction, by merciless, wild and voracious beasts. Though the children were saucy, yet a man of any considerable candor, would have made allowance for their non-age, " for childhood and youth are vanity." " And he went up from thence unto Bethel, and as he was going up by the way, there came forth little children out of the city and mocked him, and said unto him, go up thou bald-head, go up thou bald-

head, and he turned back and looked on them, and he
cursed them in the name of the Lord, and there came forth
two she bears out of the wood, and tare forty and two
children of them." It seems by the children's address
to Elisha, that he was an old bald-headed man, and that
they had heard, that his mate, Elijah, had gone up a little
before ; and as it was an uncommon thing for men to
kite away into the air, and leave the world after that sort,
it is likely that it excited a curiosity in the children to
see Elisha go off with himself in the same manner, which
occasioned their particular mode of speech to him, saying,
" go up bald head." The writings of Solomon, King of
Israel, must needs have been foisted into the canonical
volume by some means or other, for no one passage
therein gives the least intimation of inspiration, or that
he had any immediate dictation from God in his compositions, but on the contrary, he informs us, that he acquired his knowledge by applying himself to wisdom, " to
seek and to search out concerning all things that are done
under the sun. This sore travail," says he, " has God
given to the sons of men to be exercised therewith." And
since Solomon never pretended to inspiration, others cannot justly claim his writings to have been anything
more than natural reasonings, for who can, with propriety stamp his writings with divine authority, when he
pretended no such thing, but the contrary? His song of
songs appears to be rather of the amorous kind, and is
supposed to have been written at the time he was making
love to the daughter of Pharaoh, King of Egypt, who is
said to have been a princess of exquisite beauty and
exceeding coy, and so captivated his affections that it

made him light headed and sing about the "*joints of her thighs*," and her " *belly.*"

The divine legation of Moses and the prophets is rendered questionable from the consideration that they never taught the doctrine of immortality, their rewards and punishments are altogether temporary, terminating at death ; they have not so much as exhibited any speculation of surviving the grave ; to this is ascribed the unbelief of the Sadducees of the resurection of the dead, or of an angel or spirit, as they strenuously adhered to the law of Moses, for they could not imagine, but that their great prophet and law giver would have apprised them of a state of immortality had it been true ; and in this the Sadducees seem to argue with force on their position of the divine legation of Moses. For admitting the reality of man's immortality, it appears incredible to suppose, that God should have specially commissioned Moses, as his prophet and instructor to the tribes of Israel, and not withal to have instructed them in the important doctrine of a future existence.

.5 *

SECTION III.

DREAMS OR VISIONS UNCERTAIN AND CHIMERICAL CHANNEL
FOR THE CONVEYANCE OF REVELATION ; WITH REMARKS
ON THE COMMUNICATION OF THE HOLY GHOST TO THE
DISCIPLES, BY THE PRAYERS AND LAYING ON OF THE
APOSTLES HANDS, WITH OBSERVATIONS ON THE DIVINE
DICTATIONS OF THE FIRST PROMULGATORS OF THE GOSPEL,
AND AN ACCOUNT OF THE ELECT LADY, AND HER NEW
SECTARY OF SHAKERS.

It appears from the writings of the prophets and
apostles, that part of their revelations were communicated
to them by dreams and visions, which have no other existence but in the imagination, and are defined to be " the
images which appear to the mind during sleep, figuratively,
a chimera, a groundless fancy or conceit, without reason."
Our experience agrees with this definition, and evinces
that there is no trust to be reposed in them. They are
fictitious images of the mind, not under the control of
the understanding, and therefore not regarded at this day
except by the credulous and superstitious, who still retain
a veneration for them. But that a revelation from God
to man, to be continued to the latest posterity as a divine
and perfect rule of duty or law, should be communicated
through such a fictitious and chimerical channel, carries
with it the evident marks of deception itself, or of unintelligibleness, as appears from the vision of St. Paul.
" It is not expedient for me doubtless to glory, I will
come to visions and revelations of the Lord ; I knew a
man in Christ above fourteen years ago, whether in the
body I cannot tell, or whether out of the body I
cannot tell, God knoweth such an one caught up to

the third heavens. And I knew such a man, whether in the body or out of the body I cannot tell, God knoweth how that he was caught up into Paradise and heard unspeakable words which it is not lawful for a man to utter." That God knoweth the whole affair, will not be disputed, but that we should understand it is impossible, for the apostle's account of his vision is unintelligible; it appears that he was rather in a delirium or a stupor, so that he knew not that whether he was in or out of the body: he says he heard " *unspeakable words,*" but this communicates no intelligence of the subject-matter of them to us; and that they " *were not lawful for a man to utter,*" but what they were, or wherein their unlawfulness to be uttered by man consisted, he does not inform us. His revelation from his own story was unspeakable and unlawful, and so he told us nothing what it was, nor does it compose any part of revelation, which is to *make known.* He is explicit as to his being caught up to the third heaven, but how he could understand that is incredible, when at the same time he knew not whether he was in the body or out of the body; and if he was in such a delirium that he did not know so domestic a matter as that, it is not to be supposed that he could be a competent judge whether he was at the first, second, third, or fourth heaven, or whether he was advanced above the surface of the earth, or not.

That the apostles in their ministry were dictated by the Holy Ghost, in the settlement of disputable doctrines, is highly questionable. " Forasmuch as we have heard that certain, which went out from us have troubled you with words, subverting your souls, saying, ye must be circumcised and keep the law, to whom we gave no such commandment, for it seemed good to the Holy Ghost, and to us, to lay upon you no other burden than these necessary things." Acts 15. And after having given a history of the disputations concerning circumcision, and of keeping the law of Moses, and of the result of the council, the same chapter informs us, that a contention happened so sharp between Paul and Barnabas, " that they parted asunder the one from the other." Had the Holy Ghost been the dictator of the first teachers of Christianity, as individuals, there could have been no disputable doctrines or controversies, respecting the religion which they were promulgating in the world or in the manner of doing it, to be referred to a general council of the apostles and elders held at Jerusalem," for had they been directed by the Holy Ghost, there could have been no controversies among them to have referred to the council. And inasmuch as the Holy Ghost neglected them as individuals, why is it not as likely that it neglected to dictate the council held at Jerusalem or elsewhere ? It seems that the Holy Ghost no otherwise directed them in their plan of religion, than by the general council of the apostles and elders, the same as all other communities are governed. " Paul having passed through the upper coasts came to Ephesus, and finding certain disciples, he said unto them have ye received the Holy Ghost since ye believed ? and they said unto him we have not so much as heard whether there be any Holy Ghost ; and when Paul had laid his hands upon them, the Holy Ghost came on them, and they spoke with tongues and prophesied."

The spirit of God is that which constitutes the divine

essence, and makes him to be what he is, but that he should be dictated, or his spirit be communicated by any acts or ceremonies of the apostles, is by no means admissible; for such exertions of the apostles, so far as they may be supposed to communicate the holy spirit to their disciples, would have made God passive in the premised act of the gift of the spirit; for it must have been either the immediate act of God or of the apostles, and if it was the immediate act of the one, it could not have been the immediate act of the other.

To suppose that the act of the gift of the spirit was the mere act of God, and at the same time the mere act of the apostles, are propositions diametrically opposed to each other, and cannot both be true. But it may be supposed that the gift of the spirit was partly the act of God and partly the act of the apostles; admitting this to have been the case the consequences would follow, that the act of the gift of the spirit was partly divine and partly human, and therefore the beneficence and glory of the grant of the gift of the spirit unto the disciples, would belong partly to God and partly to the apostles, and in an exact proportion to that which God and they may be supposed to have respectively contributed towards the marvellous act of the gift of the spirit. But that God should act in partnership with man, or share his providence and glory with him, is too absurd to demand argumentative confutation, especially in an act which immediately respects the display or exertion of the divine spirit on the spirits of men.

Such delusions have taken place in every age of the world since history has attained to any considerable

110ORACLES OF REASON.

degree of intelligence ; nor is there at present a nation on earth, but what is more or less infatuated with delusory notions of the immediate influence of good or evil spirits on their minds. A recent instance of it appears in the Elect Lady (as she has seen fit to style herself) and her followers, called Shakers ; this pretended holy woman began her religious scheme at Connestaguna ; in the northwestardly part of the State of New. York, about the year 1769, and has added a new sectary to the religious catalogue. After having instilled her tenets among the Connestagunites, and the adjacent inhabitants, she rambled into several parts of the country, promulgating her religion, and has gained a considerable number of scattering proselytes, not only in the State of New York, but some in the New England States. She has so wrought on the minds of her female devotees, respecting the fading nature, vanity and tempting allurements of their ornaments (which by the by are not plenty among her followers,) and the deceitfulness of riches, that she has procured from them a considerable number of strings of gold beads and jewels, and amassed a small treasure ; and like most sectaries engrosses the kingdom of heaven to herself and her followers, to the seclusion of all others. She gives out that her mission is immediately from heaven, that she travails in pain for her elect, and pretends to talk in seventy-two unknown languages, in which she converses with those who have departed this life, and says, that there has not been a true church on earth since the apostles days until she had erected hers. That both the living and the dead must be saved in, by, and through her, and that they must confess their sins unto her and procure her pardon, or cannot be saved. That every of the human race who have died since the apostle's time, until her church was set up has been damned, and that they are continually making intercession to her for salvation, which is the occasion of her talking to them in those unknown tongues ; and that she gathers her elect from earth and hell. She wholly refuses to give a reason for what she does or says : but says that it is the duty of mankind to believe in her, and receive her instructions, for they are infallible.

For a time she prohibited her disciples from propagating their species, but soon after gave them ample license, restricting them, indiscriminately, to the pale of her sanctified church, for that she nedeed more souls to complete the number of her elect. Among other things, she instructs those who are young and sprightly among her pupils, to practise the most wild, freakish, wanton and romantic gestures, as to that of indecently stripping themselves, twirling round, extorting their features, shaking and twitching their bodies and limbs into a variety of odd and unusual ways, and many other extravagancies of external behavior, in the practice of which they are said to be very alert even to the astonishment of spectators, having by use acquired an uncommon agility in such twirling, freakish and romantic practices. The old Lady having such an ascendancy over them as to make them believe that those extravagant actions were occasioned by the immediate power of God, it serves among them as a proof of the divinity of her doctrines.

A more particular account of this new sectary has been

lately published in a pamphlet by a Mr. Rathburn, who, as he relates, was for a time, one of her deluded disciples, but after a while apostatised from the faith, and has since announced to the world the particulars of their doctrine and conduct.

Probably there never was any people or country, since the era of historical knowledge, who were more confident than they that they are acted upon by the immediate agency of the divine spirit; and as there are facts now existing in a considerable tract of country, and are notoriously known in this part of America, I take the liberty to mention them, as a knowledge of these facts, together with the concurrent testimony of the history of such deceptions in all ages and nations, might induce my countrymen to examine strictly into the claim and reality of ghostly intelligence in general.

CHAPTER VIII.

SECTION I.

OF THE NATURE OF FAITH AND WHEREIN IT CONSISTS.

Faith in Jesus Christ and in his Gospel throughout the New Testament, is represented to be an essential condition of the eternal salvation of mankind. " Knowing that a man is not justified by the works of the law, but by the faith of Jesus Christ, even we have believed in Jesus Christ, that we might be justified by the faith of Christ, and not by the works of the law, for by the works of the law shall no flesh be justified." Again, " If thou shalt confess the Lord Jesus Christ, and believe in thine heart that God hath raised him from the dead, thou mayst be saved." And again, "He that believeth and is baptized shall be saved, but he that believeth not shall be damned." Faith is the last result of the understanding, or the same which we call the conclusion, it is the consequence of a greater or less deduction of reasoning from certain premises previously laid down ; it is the same as believing or judging of any matter of fact, or assenting to or dissenting from the truth of any doctrine, system or position ; so that to form a judgment, or to come to a determination in one's own mind, or to believe, or to have faith, is in reality the same thing, and is synonymously applied both in writing and speaking, for example, "Abraham believed in God." Again, "for he," speaking of Abraham, "judged him faithful who had promised," and again "his faith was counted unto him for righteousness." It is not only in scripture that we meet with examples of the three words, to wit, belief, judgment, and faith, to stand for the marks of our ideas for the same thing, but also all intelligible writers'and speakers apply these phrases synonymously, and it would be good grammar and sense, for us to say that we have faith in a universal providence, or that we judge that there is a universal providence. These three · different phrases, in communicating our ideas of providence, do every one of them exhibit the same idea, to all persons of common understanding, who are acquainted with the English language. In fine, every one's experience may convince them that they cannot assent to, or dissent from the truth of any matter of fact, doctrine or proposition whatever, contrary to their judgment ; for the act of the mind in assenting to or dissenting from any position, or in having faith or belief in favor of, or against any doctrine, system, or proposition, could not amount to anything more or less, than the act of the judgment, or last dictate of the understanding, whether the understanding be supposed to be rightly informed or not: so that our faith in all cases is as liable to err, as our reason is to misjudge of the truth ; and our minds act faith in disbelieving any doctrine or system of religion to be true, as much as in believing it to be so. From hence it appears, that the mind cannot act faith in opposition to its judgment, but that it is the resolution of the understanding itself committed to memory or writing, and can never be considered distinct from it. And inasmuch as faith necessarily results from reasoning, forcing itself upon our minds by the evidence of truth, or the mistaken apprehension of it, without any act of choice of ours, there cannot be any thing, which pertains to, or partakes of the nature of moral good or evil in it. For us to believe such doctrines, or systems of religion, as appears to be credibly recommended to our reason, can no more partake of the nature of goodness or morality, than our natural eyes may be supposed to partake of it in their perception of colors ; for the faith of the mind, and the sight of the eye are both of them necessary consequences, the one results from the reasonings of the mind, and the other from the perception of the eye. To suppose a rational mind without the exercise of faith would be as absurd as to suppose a proper and complete eye without sight, or the perception of the common objects of that sense. The short of the matter is this, that without reason we could not have faith, and without the eye or eyes we could not see, but once admitting that we are rational, faith follows of course, naturally resulting from the dictates of reason..

SECTION II.

OF THE TRADITIONS OF OUR FOREFATHERS.

It may be objected, that the far greater part of mankind believe according to the tradition of their forefathers, without examining into the grounds of it, and that argumentative deductions from the reason and nature of things, have, with the bulk of them, but little or no influence on their faith. Admitting 'this to have been too much the case, and that many of them have been blameable for the omission of cultivating or improving their reason, and for not forming a better judgment concerning their respective traditions, or a juster and more exalted faith ; yet this does not at all invalidate the foregoing arguments respecting the nature of faith : for though it be admitted that most of the human race do not, or will not reason, with any considerable degree of propriety, on the traditions of their forefathers, but receive them implicitly, they nevertheless establish this one proposition in their minds, right or wrong, *that their respective traditions are right*, for none could believe in them were they possessed of the knowledge that they were wrong. And as we have a natural bias in favor of our progenitors, to whose memory a tribute of regard is justly due, and whose care

in handing down from father to son such notions of
religion and manners, as they supposed would be for the·
well being and happiness of their posterity in this and
the coming world, naturally endears tradition to us, and
prompts us to receive and venerate it.   Add to this, that
the priests of every denomination are *" instant in season
and out of season,"* in inculcating and instilling the same
tenets, which, with the foregoing considerations, induces
mankind in general to give at least a tacit consent to
their respective traditions, and without a thorough inves-
tigation thereof, believe them to be right and very commonly infallible, although their examinations are not
attended with argumentative reasonings, from the nature
of things ; and in the same proportion as they may be·
supposed to fall short of conclusive arguing on their
respective traditions they cannot fail to be deceived in the
rationality of their faith.

   But after all it may be that some of the human race
may have been traditionally or accidentally right, in many
or most respects.   Admitting it to be so, yet they cannot
have any rational enjoyment of it, or understand wherein
the truth of the premised right tradition consists, or
deduce any more satisfaction from it, than others whose
traditions may be supposed to be wrong ; for it is the
knowledge of the discovery of truth alone, which is
gratifying to that mind who contemplates its superlative
beauty.

   That tradition has had a powerful influence on the
human mind is universally admitted, even by those who
are governed by it in the articles or discipline of their
faith ; for though they are blind with respect to their own

superstition, yet they can perceive and despise it in others. Protestants very readily discern and expose the weak side of Popery, and Papists are as ready and acute in discovering the errors of heretics.   With equal facility do Christians and Mahometans spy out each others inconsistencies and both have an admirable sagacity to descry the superstition of the heathen nations.   Nor are the Jews wholly silent in this matter ; "O God the heathen are come into thine inheritance, thy holy temple have they defiled."   What abomination must this have been in the opinion of a nation who had monopolized all religion to themselves!   Monstrous vile heathen, that they should presume to approach the *sanctum sanctorum!*   The Christians call the Mahometans by the odious name of infidels, but the Musslemen, in their opinion, cannot call the Christians by a worse name than that which they have given themselves, they therefore call them *Christians*.

What has been already observed upon tradition, is sufficient to admonish us of its errors and superstitions, and the prejudices to which a bigoted attachment thereto exposes us, which is abundantly sufficient to excite us to a careful examination of our respective traditions, and not to rest satisfied until we have regulated our faith by reason.

SECTION III.

OUR FAITH IS GOVERNED BY OUR REASONINGS, WHETHER
THEY ARE SUPPOSED TO BE CONCLUSIVE OR INCONCLUSIVE,
AND NOT MERELY BY OUR OWN CHOICE.

It is written that " Faith is the gift of God."   Be it
so, but is faith any more the gift of God than reflection,
memory or reason are his gifts ?   Was it not for memory,
we could not retain in our minds the judgment which we
have passed upon things ; and was it not for reasoning,
in either a regular or irregular manner, or partly both,
there could be no such thing as judging or believing ;
so that God could not bestow the gift of faith separate
from the gift of reason, faith being the mere consequence
of reasoning, either right or wrong, or in a greater or less
degree, as has been previously argued.

Still there is a knotty text of scripture to surmount,
viz : " He that believeth shall be saved, but he that
believeth not shall be damned."   This text is considered
as crowding hard upon unbelievers in christianity ; but
when it is critically examined, it will be found not to
militate at all against them, but is merely a Jesuitical
fetch to overawe some and make others wonder.   We will
premise, that an unbeliever is destitute of faith, which
is the cause of his being thus denominated.   The Christian
believes the gospel to be true and of divine authority,
the Deist believes that it is not true and not of divine
authority ; so that the Christian and Deist are both of
them believers, and according to the express words of the
text, " shall be saved," and a Deist may as well retort

upon a Christian and call him an infidel, because he differs in faith from him, as a Christian may upon the Deist; for there is the same impropriety in applying the cant of infidelity to either, as both are believers; and it is impossible for us to believe contrary to our judgments or the dictates of understanding, whether it be rightly informed or not. Why then may there not in both denominations be honest men, who are seeking after the truth, and who may have an equal right to expect the favor and salvation of God.

CHAPTER IX.

SECTION I.

A TRINITY OF PERSONS CANNOT EXIST IN THE DIVINE ESSENCE WHETHER THE PERSONS BE SUPPOSED TO BE FINITE OR INFINITE: WITH REMARKS ON ST. ATHANA-SIUS'S CREED.

OF all errors which have taken place in religion, none have been so fatal to it as those that immediately respect the divine nature. Wrong notions of a God, or of his providence, sap its very foundation in theory and prac-tice, as is evident from the superstition discoverable among the major part of mankind; who, instead of wor-shipping the true God, have been by some means or other infatuated to pay divine homage to *mere creatures*, or to idols made with hands, or to such as have no exist-ence but in their own fertile imaginations.

God being incomprehensible to us, we cannot under-

stand all that perfection in which the divine essence consists, we can nevertheless (negatively) comprehend many
things, in which (positively) the divine essence does not
and cannot consist.

That it does not consist of three persons, or of any
other number of persons, is as easily demonstrated, as
that the *whole* is *bigger* than a *part*, or any other proposition in mathematics.

We will premise, that the three persons in the supposed Trinity are either finite or infinite; for there cannot in the scale of being be a third sort of beings between
these two; for ever so many and exalted degrees in
finiteness is still finite, and that being who is infinite admits of no degrees of enlargement; and as all beings whatever must be limited or unlimited, perfect or imperfect,
they must therefore be denominated to be finite or infinite : we will therefore premise the three persons in the
Trinity to be merely finite, considered personally and
individually from each other, and the question would
arise whether the supposed Trinity of finites though
united in one essence, could be more than finite still.
Inasmuch as three imperfect and circumscribed beings
united together could not constitute a being perfect or
infinite, any more than absolute perfection could consist
of three imperfections ; which would be the same as to
suppose that infinity could be made up or compounded
of finiteness ; or that absolute, uncreated and infinite
perfection, could consist of three personal and imperfect
natures.   But on the other hand, to consider every of
the three persons in the supposed Trinity, as being absolutely infinite, it would be a downright contradiction to

one infinite and all comprehending essence. Admitting that God the Father is infinite, it would necessarily preclude the supposed God the Son, and God the Holy Ghost from the god-head, or essence of God; one infinite essence comprehending every power, excellency and perfection, which can possibly exist in the divine nature. Was it possible that three absolute infinites, which is the same as three Gods, could be contained in one and the self-same essence, why not as well any other number of infinites? But as certain as infinity cannot admit of addition, so certain a plurality of infinites cannot exist in the same essence; for real infinity is strict and absolute infinity, and only that, and cannot be compounded of infinities or of parts, but forecloses all addition. A personal or circumscribed God, implies as great and manifest a contradiction as the mind of man can conceive of; it is the same as a limited omnipresence, a weak Almighty, or a finite God.

From the foregoing arguments on the Trinity, we infer, that the divine essence cannot consist of a Trinity of persons, whether they are supposed to be either finite or infinite.

The creed-mongers have exhibited the doctrine of the Trinity in an alarming point of light, viz.: "Whoever would be saved before all things it is necessary that he hold the Catholic faith, which faith, except every one doth keep whole and undefiled, without doubt he shall perish everlastingly." We next proceed to the doctrine, "The Father is eternal, the Son is eternal, and the Holy Ghost is eternal, and yet there are not three eternals but one eternal." The plain English is, that the three persons in the Trinity are three eternals, individually considered, and yet they are not three eternals but one eternal.

To say that there are three eternals in the Trinity, and yet that there are not three eternals therein, is a contradiction in terms, as much as to say, that there are three persons in the Trinity and yet there are not three persons in the Trinity.

The first proposition in the creed affirms, that "the Father is eternal," the second affirms that "the Son is eternal," the third affirms that "the Holy Ghost is eternal," the fourth affirms that "there are not three eternals," and the fifth that there is "but one eternal."

The reader will observe, that the three first propositions are denied by the fourth, which denies that there are three eternals, though the three first propositions affirmed, that there were three eternals by name, viz. the Father, Son and Holy Ghost. The fifth proposition is unconnected with either of the former, and is undoubtedly true, viz. "but there is one eternal." "The Father is God, the Son is God, and the Holy Ghost is God, and yet there are not three Gods but one God." Here again we have three Gods by name, affirmed to have an existence by the three first propositions, by the fourth they are negatived, and the fifth affirms the truth again, viz. that there is "but one God."

Admitting the three first propositions to be true, to wit, that there are three Gods, the three could not be one and the same God, any more than Diana, Dagan and Moloch may be supposed to be the same; and if three Gods, their essences and providences would interfere and make universal confusion and disorder.

" The Father is Almighty, the Son is Almighty, and the Holy Ghost is Almighty, and yet there are not three Almighties but one Almighty." Here we have three Almighties and at the same time but one Almighty. So that the point at issue is brought to this simple question, viz. whether three units can be one, or one unit three or .not? Which is submitted to the curious to determine. Our creed further informs us, that the three persons in the Trinity are co-eternal together and co-equal, but in its sequel we are told that one was begotten of the other; and when we advert to the history of that trans-action, we find it to be not quite eighteen hundred years ago, and took place in the reign of Herod, the King of Judea, which faith except " we keep whole and unde-filed," we have a threat, that " without doubt we shall perish everlastingly."'

SECTION II.

ESSENCE BEING THE CAUSE OF IDENTITY, IS INCONSIST-
ENT WITH PERSONALITY IN THE DIVINE NATURE.

ONE God can have but one essence, which must have been eternal and infinite, and for that reason precludes all others from a participation of his nature, glory, and universal and absolute perfection.

When we speak of any being who by nature is capa-ble of being rightfully denominated an individual, we conceive of it to exist but in one essence ; so that essence as applied to God, denominates the divine nature ; and as applied to man, it denotes an individual : for although the human race is with propriety denominated the race of man, and though every male of the species, is with equal propriety called man, for that they partake of one common sort of nature and likeness, yet the respective individuals are not one and the same.   The person of A is not the person of B, nor are they conscious of each other's consciousness, and therefore the joy or grief of A, is not and cannot be the joy or grief of B; this is what we know to be a fact from our own experience. The reason of this personal distinction is founded in nature, for though we partake of one common nature and likeness, yet we do not partake of one and the same essence. Essence is therefore, in the order of nature, the primary cause of identity or sameness and cannot be divided.

From hence we infer, that the doctrine of the Trinity is destitute of foundation, and tends manifestly to superstition and idolatry.

SECTION III.

THE IMPERFECTION OF KNOWLEDGE IN THE PERSON OF JESUS CHRIST, INCOMPATIBLE WITH HIS DIVINITY.

THAT Jesus Christ was not God is evident from his own words, where, speaking of the day of judgment, he says, " Of that day and hour knoweth no man, no not the angels which are in Heaven, neither the Son, but the Father." This is giving up all pretention to divinity, acknowledging in the most explicit manner, that he did not know all things, but compares his understanding to that of man and angels ; " of that day and hour knoweth no man, no not the angels which are in heaven, neither the Son." Thus he ranks himself with finite beings, and with them acknowledges, that he did not know the day and hour of judgment, and at the same time ascribes a superiority of knowledge to the father, for that he knew the day and hour of judgment.

That he was a mere creature is further evident from his prayer to the father, saying, " father if it be possible, let this cup pass from me, nevertheless, not my will but thine be done." These expressions speak forth the most humble submission to his father's will, authority and government, and however becoming so submissive a disposition to the divine government would be, in a creature, it is utterly inconsistent and unworthy of a God, or of the person of Jesus Christ, admitting him to have been a divine person, or of the essence of God.

CHAPTER X.

SECTION I.

OBSERVATIONS ON THE STATE OF MAN, IN MOSES'S PAR-
ADISE, ON THE TREE OF KNOWLEDGE OF GOOD AND
EVIL, AND ON THE TREE OF LIFE : WITH SPECULA-
TIONS ON THE DIVINE PROHIBITION TO MAN, NOT TO
EAT OF THE FRUIT OF THE FORMER OF THOSE TREES,
INTERSPERSED WITH REMARKS ON THE MORTALITY OF
INNOCENT MAN.

THE mortality of animal life, and the dissolution of
that of the vegetable, has been particularly considered in
chapter three, section four, treating on physical evils.
We now proceed to make an application of those arguments, in the case of our reputed first parents, whose
mortality is represented by Moses to have taken place in
consequence of their eating of the forbidden fruit.

Moses in his description of the garden of Eden acquaints us with two chimerical kinds of fruit trees, which,
among others, he tells us were planted by God in the
place appointed for the residence of the new made couple ;
the one he calls by the name of " the tree of knowledge
of good and evil," and the other by the name of " the
tree of life." And previous to his account of the apostacy, he informs us, that God expressly commanded the
man and woman, saying, " be fruitful and multiply and
replenish the earth and subdue it, and have dominion
over the fish of the sea, and over the fowl of the air,
and over every living thing that moveth upon the earth ;
and God said, behold I have given you every herb bear-

ing seed, which is upon the face of all the earth, and every tree, in which is the fruit of a tree yielding seed, to you it shall be for meat." Again, "and the Lord commanded the man saying, of every tree of the garden thou mayest freely eat, but of the tree of knowledge of good and evil thou shalt not eat of it, for in the day that thou eatest thereof thou shalt surely die." "And the Lord said, it is not good for man to be alone, I will make him an help meet for him; and the Lord God caused a deep sleep to fall upon Adam, and he slept, and he took out one of his ribs, and closed up the flesh instead thereof, and the rib which the Lord God had taken from man made he a woman.

Thus it appears from Moses's representation of the state of man's innocency, that he was commanded by God to labor, and to replenish the earth; and that to him was given the dominion over the creatures, and that at two several times he was licensed by God himself to eat of every of the fruit of the trees, and of the herbage, except of the tree of knowledge of good and evil; and because it was not good that the man should be alone, but that he might multiply and replenish the earth, our amorous mother Eve, it seems, was formed, who I dare say well compensated father Adam for the loss of his rib.

This short description of man's state and condition in innocency, agrees with the state and circumstances of human nature at present. Innocent man was required to labor and subdue the earth, out of which he was to be subsisted; had a license to eat of the fruit of the trees, or herbage of the garden, which pre-supposeth,

that his nature needed refreshment the same as ours
does ; for otherwise it would have been impertinent to
have granted him a privilege incompatible with his
nature, as it would have been no privilege at all, but an
outright mockery, except we admit, that innocent human
nature was liable to decay, needed nutrition by food, and
had the quality of digestion and perspiration ; or in fine,
had the same sort of nature as we have ; for otherwise
he could eat but one belly-full, which without digestion
would remain the same, and is too romantic to have been
the original end and design of eating. And though
there is nothing mentioned by Moses concerning his
drinking, yet it is altogether probable, that he had wit
enough to drink when he was thirsty. That he consisted
of animal nature is manifest, not only from his being
subjected to subdue the earth, out of which he was to be
subsisted, and from his eating and drinking, or his susceptibility of nutrition by food, but also from his pro-
pensity to propagate his kind ; for which purpose a help-
mate was made for him.

Nothing could more fully evince, that Moses's innocent progenitors of mankind, in that state, were of a
similar nature to ours, than their susceptibility of propagating the species ; and as they required nutrition, their
nature must have had the quality or aptitude of digestion
and perspiration, and every property that at present we
ascribe to an animal nature ; from hence we infer, that
death, or mortality, must have been the necessary consequence. What would have prevented them from having
been crushed to death by a fall from a precipice, or from
uffering death by any other casualty, to which human

nature is at present liable? will any suppose that the bodies of those premised innocent progenitors of the human race were invulnerable; were they not flesh and blood? surely they were, for otherwise they could not have been male and 'female; as it was written, "male and female created he them:" and inasmuch as animal life has, from its original, consisted of the same sort of nature, and been propagated and supported in the same manner, and obnoxious to the same fate, it would undoubtedly, in the premised day of Adam, required the same order in the external system of nature, which it does at present, to answer the purposes of animal life.

Was it possible that the laws of nature, which merely respect gravitation, could be and were suspended, so as not to be influential on matter, our world would be immediately disjointed and out of order, and confusion would succeed its present regularity; in the convulsions whereof animal life could not subsist. So that not only the laws which immediately respect animal nature in particular, but the laws which respect our solar system, must have been the same in man's innocency, as in his whimsically supposed state of apostacy; and consequently, his mortality the same. From hence we infer, that the curses, which Moses informs us of in chapter three: as being by God pronounced upon man, saying, "dust thou art, and unto dust thou shalt return," could not have been any punishment, inflicted as a penalty for eating the forbidden fruit; for turn to dust he must have done, whether he eat of it or not; for that death and dissolution was the inevitable and irreversible condition of the law of nature, which wholly precludes the curse,

6 *

of which Moses informs us, from having any effect on mankind.

The story of the "tree of life," is unnatural. And there being but one of the kind, it may be called an only tree, the world not having produced another of the sort; the fruit of which, according to Moses, had such an effi- cacious quality, that had Adam and Eve but eaten thereof, they would have lived forever. "And now lest he put forth his hand and take also of the tree of life, and eat, and live forever." To prevent which, they are said to be driven out of the garden, that the eating thereof might not have reversed the sentence of God, which he had previously pronounced against them, denouncing their mortality. "So he drove out the man, and he placed at the east of the garden of Eden, cherubims, and a flaming sword, which turneth every way to keep the way of the tree of life." A bite of this fruit it seems would have reinstated mankind, and spoiled priestcraft. Yet it is observable, that there are no travellers or histo- rians, who have given any accounts of such a tree, or of the cherubims or flaming sword, which renders its exist- ence disputable, and the reality of it doubtful and im- probable ; the more so, as that part of the country, in which it is said to have been planted, has for a long suc- cession of ages been populously inhabited.

Yet it may be objected, that the tree may have rotted down and consumed by time. But such conjectures derogate from the character of the quality of the tree. It seems, that so marvellous a tree, the fruit of which would have preserved animal life eternally, would have laughed at time, and id defiance to decay and dissolution, and eternally have remained in its pristine state under the protection of the flaming sword, as a perpetual evidence of the divine legation of Moses, and the reality of man's apostacy for ever. But alas! it is no where to be found, it is perished from off the face of the earth, and such a marvellous fruit is no more, and consequently no remedy against mortality remains.

SECTION II.

POINTING OUT THE NATURAL IMPOSSIBILITY OF ALL AND EVERY OF THE DIVERSE SPECIES OF BIPED ANIMALS, COMMONLY TERMED MAN, TO HAVE LINEALLY DE- SCENDED FROM ADAM AND EVE, OR FROM THE SAME ORIGINAL PROGENITORS.

It is altogether improbable and manifestly contradictory to suppose, that the various and diverse nations and tribes of the earth, who walk upon two legs, and are included under the term *man*, have or possibly could have descended by ordinary generation, from the same parents, be they supposed to be who they will.

Those adventurers, who have sailed or travelled to the several parts of the globe, inform us, in their respective histories, that they find the habitable part of it more or less populated by one kind or other of rational animals, and that considered as tribes or nations, there is evidently a gradation of intellectual capacity among them, some more exalted and others lower in the scale of being; and that they are specially diverse from each other with respect to their several animal natures, though

-in most respects they appear to have one sort of nature
with us, viz : more like us that like the brute creation ;
as they walk erect, speak with man's voice, and make use
of language of one sort or other, though many of them
are more or less inarticulate in their manner of speaking :
and in many other particulars bear a general likeness to
us.   They are nevertheless considered as distinct tribes
or nations, are of different sizes, and as to complexion,
they vary from the two extremes of white and black, in
a variety of tawny mediums.

The learned nations can trace their genealogies, (though
somewhat incorrect) for a considerable time, but are certain to be sooner or later lost in the retrospect thereon,
and those that are of an inferior kind, or destitute of
learning or science have no other knowledge of their
genealogies, than they retain by their respective traditions,
which are very inconsiderable.   They are likewise diverse from each other in their features and in the shape
of their bodies and limbs, and some are distinguished
from others by their rank smell and the difference in their
hair, eyes and visage, but to point out the distinctions
would exceed my design.

The Ethiopians, though of a shining black complexion,
have regular and beautiful features, and long black hair
(one of those female beauties captivated the affections of
Moses) they differ very materially from the negro blacks,
so that it appears impossible that they should have descended in a lineal succession from the same ancestors.
They are uniformly in their respective generations essentially diverse from each other, so that an issue from a
male and female of the two nations would be a mongrel,

partaking partly of the kind of both nations. So also concerning the difference which subsists between us and the negroes; their black skin is but one of the particulars in which they are different from us; their many and very essential differences fully evince, that the white nations, and they, could not according to the law of their respective generations, have had one and the same lineal original, but that they have had their diverse kind of original progenitors.

It is true that the several nations and tribes of the earth, comprehended under the general term man, notwithstanding their diversity to each other in bodily shape and mental powers, bear a nearer resemblance to one another than the brute kind, for which reason they are known by one common appellation: though it is manifest that they could never have lineally descended from the same first parents, whether their names were Adam and Eve, or what not.

But inasmuch as our genealogies are wholly insufficient for the purpose of explaining our respective originals or any or either of them, or to give us or any of us, considered as individuals or nations, who fall under the denomination of the term man, any manner of insight or knowledge from whom we are lineally descended, or who were our respective original ancestors, or what their names were: we must therefore reason on this subject from the facts and causes now existing, which abundantly evince, that we are of different kinds, and consequently are not of the same lineage.

The acquaintance, which we have had with the negro nation in particular, fully evinces the absurdity of supposing them to be of the same blood and kindred with ourselves. But that there are some original intrinsic and hereditary diversity or essential difference between us and them, which cannot be ascribed to time, climate, or to mere contingence.

For that we and they are in nature inherently and uniformly diverse from each other in our respective constitutions and generations, and have been so time immemorial. So that the negroes are of a different species of rational beings from us, and consequently must have had their distinct lineal original; was it not so, there could be no such thing as a mongrel or a mulatto, who is occasioned by a copulation between the males and the females of the respective diverse species, the issue partaking of both natures.

Had all the nations and tribes of the world, who are denominated rational, been lineally descended from the same progenitors, mongrelism could never have taken place among them, as in this case they would have been all of the same kind : from hence we infer, that they have had their respective original progenitors. The Dutch colony at the Cape of Good Hope have enacted laws to punish with death such of their Dutch subjects as may be convicted of copulating with the Hottentots : for that their nature is adjusted to be of an inferior species to theirs, so that mixing their nature with them would essentially degenerate and debase their own.

SECTION III.

OF THE ORIGIN OF THE DEVIL OR OF MORAL EVIL, AND
OF THE DEVIL'S TALKING WITH EVE ; WITH A RE-
MARK THAT THE DOCTRINE OF APOSTACY IS THE
FOUNDATION OF CHRISTIANITY.

INASMUCH as the devil is represented to have had so
great and undue an influence in bringing about the apostacy of Adam, and still to continue his temptations to
mankind, it may be worth our while to examine into the
nature and manner of his being and the mode of his
exhibiting his temptations.

John's gospel, verse 1 and 3, the Christian's God is
the creator of the devil and consequently the original
cause of evil in heaven — and among men he planted
the tree of knowledge of good and evil, and knew at the
time he planted it of the awful consequences that would
follow.

But if it be admitted, that the creature called the devil
(who must be supposed to be under the divine government, as much as any other creature) could become in-
flexible, and perpetually rebellious and wicked, incapable
of a restoration, and consequently subjected to eternal
punishment (which to me appears to be inconsistent with
the wisdom and goodness of the divine government, and
the nature, end and design of a probationary agent) yet
it would by no means follow from hence, that so stub-
bornly wicked and incorrigible a creature would have
been permitted, by the providence of God, to tempt,
ensnare or seduce mankind, by plying his temptations to
their weak side. One thing we are certain of, viz. that

the devil does not visit our world in a bodily or organized shape, and there is not in nature a second way, in
which it is possible for him to make known himself to
us, or that he could have done it to our progenitors, nor
could he ever have communicated to them or to us, any
temptations or ideas whatever, any otherwise than by
making a proper application to our external senses, so
that we could understand him, or receive the ideas of his
temptations in a natural way. For supernatural intercourse with the world of spirits or invisible beings has
been shown to be contradictory and impossible in the arguments contained in the sixth chapter, to which the
reader is referred. Those arguments will hold equally
good as applied to either good or evil spirits, and are
demonstrative of the utter impossibility of mankind's
holding any manner of intercourse or intelligence with
them.

But should we premise, that, according to the history
of Moses, it was in the power of the devil to assume a
bodily shape, and that he did in very deed transform
himself into the figure, likeness and organization of a
snake, yet by and with that organ he could not have
spoken or uttered the following articulate words, which
Moses charged him with, to wit, "And the serpent said
unto the woman, ye shall not surely die, for God doth
know, that in the day ye eat thereof, that your eyes shall
be opened, and ye shall be as Gods knowing good and
evil."

Who speaks the truth in the above passages, the devil,
for neither the man nor the woman died for many years
after they are said to have eaten of the forbidden fruit,

for death is the annihilation of life, and they did not die on the day they eat.

As the serpent is by nature incapable of speech, it must have put the devil into the same predicament, admitting that he transformed himself into the same figure or likeness, and consequently for want of the proper and adequate organs of speech, he must necessarily have been incapable of any other language than that of rattling his tail, and therefore could never have spoken those recited words unto Eve, or communicated any of his temptations unto her by language, while in that similitude. However, admitting that the first parents of mankind were beguiled by the wiles of the devil to transgress the divine law, yet of all transgressions it would have been the most trivial (considered under all the particular circumstances of it) that the mind of man can conceive of.

Who in the exercise of reason can believe, that Adam and Eve by eating of such a spontaneous fruit could have incurred the eternal displeasure of God, as individuals? Or that the divine vindictive justice should extend to their unoffending offspring then unborn? And sentence the human progeny to the latest posterity to everlasting destruction? As chimerical as Moses's representation of the apostacy of man manifestly appears to be, yet it is the very basis, on which Christianity is founded, and is announced in the New Testament to be the very cause why Jesus Christ came into this world, "that he might destroy the works of the devil," and redeem fallen man, alias, the elect, from the condemnation of the apostacy; which leads me to the consideration of the doctrine of imputation.

CHAPTER XI.

SECTION 1.

IMPUTATION CANNOT CHANGE, ALIENATE OR TRANSFER
THE PERSONAL DEMERIT OF SIN ; AND PERSONAL
MERIT OF VIRTUE TO OTHERS, WHO WERE NOT AC-
TIVE THEREIN, ALTHOUGH THIS DOCTRINE SUPPOSES
AN ALIENATION THEREOF.

THE doctrine of imputation according to the Christian
scheme, consists of two parts; first, of imputation of the
apostacy of Adam and Eve to their posterity, commonly
called original sin ; and secondly, of the imputation of
the merits or righteousness of Christ, who in scripture is
called the second Adam, to mankind, or to the elect.
This is a concise definition of the doctrine, and which
will undoubtedly be admitted to be a just one by every
denomination of men, who are acquainted with Christianity, whether they adhere to it or not. I therefore
proceed to illustrate and explain the doctrine by tran-
scribing a short, but very pertinent conversation, which
in the early years of my manhood, I had with a Calvin-
istical divine: but previously remark, that I was educated in what is commonly called the Armenian principles, and among other tenets to reject the doctrine of
original sin, this was the point at issue between the clergyman and me. In my turn I opposed the doctrine of
original sin with philosophical reasonings, and as I
thought had confuted the doctrine. The reverend gen-
tleman heard me through patiently, and with candor replied, " your metaphysical reasonings are not to the

purpose ; inasmuch as you are a Christian, and hope and expect to be saved by the imputed righteousness of Christ to you ; for you may as well be imputedly sinful as imputedly righteous. Nay, said he, if you hold to the doctrine of satisfaction and atonement by Christ, by so doing you pre-suppose the doctrine of apostacy or original sin to be in fact true ; for said he, if mankind were not in a ruined and condemned state by nature, there could have been no need of a redeemer, but each individual would have been accountable to his creator and judge, upon the basis of his own moral agency. Further observing, that upon philosophical principles it was difficult to account for the doctrine of original sin, or original righteousness, yet as they were plain fundamental doctrines of the Christian faith, we ought to assent to the truth of them, and that from the divine authority of revelation. Notwithstanding, said he, if you will give me a philosophical explanation of original imputed righteousness, which you profess to believe, and expect salvation by, then I will return you a philosophical explanation of the doctrine of original sin ; for it is plain, said he, that your objections lie with equal weight against original imputed righteousness, as against original imputed sin." Upon which I had the candor to acknowledge to the worthy ecclesiastic, that upon the Christian plan, I perceived that the argument had fairly terminated against me. For at that time I dared not distrust the infallibility of revelation, much more to dispute it. However, this conversation was uppermost in my mind for several months after, and after many painful searches and researches after the truth respecting the

doctrine of imputation, resolved at all events to abide the
decision of rational argument in the premises, and on a
full examination of both parts of the doctrine, rejected
the whole ; for on a fair scrutiny I found, that I must
concede to it entirely or not at all, or else believe incon-
sistently as the clergyman had argued.

Having opened and explained the doctrine, we proceed
argumentatively to consider it. Imputation of sin or
righteousness includes an alteration or transferring of
the personal merits or demerits of sin or righteousness,
from those who may be supposed to have been active in
the one or the other, to others, who are premised not to
have been active therein, otherwise it would not answer
the Bible notion of imputation. For if sin or righteousness, vice or virtue, are imputable only to their respective personal proficients or actors, in this case original sin
must have been imputed to Adam and Eve, to the exclusion of their posterity, and the righteousness of
Christ as exclusively imputed to himself, precluding all
others therefrom ; so that both the sin of the first Adam
and the righteousness of the second, would, on this
stating of imputation, have been matters which respect
merely the agency, of the demerits or merits of the two
respective Adams themselves, and in which we could
have had no blame, reward or concern, any more than in
the building of Babel.

This then is the question that determines the sequel
of the dispute for or against the doctrine of imputation,
viz. whether the personal merit or demerit of mankind,
that is to say, their virtue or vice, righteousness or wickedness can be alienated, imputed to, or transferred from

one person to another, or not? If any should object against this stating of the question now in dispute, it would be the same in reality as disputing against the doctrine of imputation itself, for imputation must transfer or change the personal merit or demerit of the sin or righteousness of mankind or not do it ; if it does not do it, the whole notion of original sin or of righteousness, as being imputed from the first and second Adams to mankind, is without foundation, consequently, if there is any reality in the doctrine of imputation, it must needs transfer or change the guilt of original sin, or of the apostacy of Adam and Eve, to their posterity, or otherwise they could need no atonement or imputative righteousness, as a remedy therefrom, but every individual of " mankind would have stood accountable to their creator and judge on the basis of their own moral agency," which is undoubted the true state of the case, respecting all rational and accountable beings ; so that if the transferring of the individual merits or demerits of one person to another, is not contained in the act or doctrine of imputation, it contains nothing at all, but is a sound without a meaning, and after all the talk which has been in the world about it, we must finally adopt to old proverb, viz. " every tub stands upon its own bottom."

SECTION II.

THE MORAL RECTITUDE OF THINGS FORECLOSES THE ACT OF IMPUTATION.

Imputation confounds virtue and vice, and saps the very foundation of moral government, both divine and human. Abstract the idea of personal merit and demerit, from the individuals of mankind, justice would be totally blind, and truth would be nullified, or at least excluded from any share in the administration of government. Admitting that moral good and evil has taken place in the system of rational agents, yet, on the position of imputation, it would be impossible, that a retribution of justice should be made to them by God or by man, except it be according to their respective personal merits and demerits; which would fix upon the basis of our own moral agency and accountability, and preclude the imputation of righteousnes.

Truth respects the reality of things, as they are in their various complicated and distinct natures, and necessarily conforms to all facts and realities. It exists in, by and with every thing that does exist, and that which does not and cannot exist, is fictitious and void of truth, as is the doctrine of imputation. It is a truth that some of the individuals of mankind are virtuous, and that others are vicious, and it is a truth, that the former merit peace of conscience and praise, and the latter horror of conscience and blame; for God has so constituted the nature of things, that moral goodness, naturally and necessarily tends to happiness in a moral sense, and moral evil as necessarily tends to the contrary; and as truth respects every thing, as being what it is, it respects nature, as God has constituted it, with its tendencies, dispositions, aptitudes and laws; and as the tendency of virtue is to mental happiness, and vice the contrary, they fall under the cognizance of truth, as all other facts necessarily do; which tendencies will for ever preclude imputation, by making us morally happy or miserable according to our works.

Truth respects the eternal rules of unalterable rectitude and fitness, which comprehends all virtue, goodness and true happiness; and as sin and wickedness is no other but a deviation from the rules of eternal unerring order and reason, so truth respects it as unreasonable, unfit, unrighteous and unhappy deviation from moral rectitude, naturally tending to misery. This order of nature, comprehended under the terms of truth, must have been of all others the wisest and best; in fine it must have been absolutely perfect; for this order and harmony of things, could not have resulted from anything short of infinite wisdom, goodness and power, by which it is also upheld; and all just ideas of equity, or of natural and moral fitness must be learned from nature, and predicated on it; and nature predicated on the immutable perfection of a God; and to suppose that imputation, in any one instance has taken place, is the same as to suppose, that the eternal order, truth, justice, equity and fitness of things has been changed, and if so, the God of nature must needs have been a changeable being, and liable to alter his justice or order of nature, which is the same thing; for without the alteration of nature, and the tendency of it, there could be no such thing as imputation, but every of the individuals of mankind would be ultimately happy or miserable, according as their respective proficiencies may be supposed to be either good or evil, agreeable to the order and tendency of nature before alluded to. For all rational and accountable agents must stand or fall upon the principles of the law of nature, except imputation alters the nature and tendency of things ; of which the immutability of a God cannot admit.

From what has been already argued on this subject, we infer, that as certain as the individuals of mankind are the proprietors of their own virtues or vices, so certain, the doctrine of imputation cannot be true. Furthermore, the supposed act or agency of imputing or transferring the personal merit or demerit of moral good or evil, *alias,* the sin of the first Adam, or the righteousness of the second Adam, to others of mankind, cannot be the act or exertion of either the first or second Adam, from whom original sin and righteousness is said to have been imputed. Nor can it be the act or doings of those individuals, to whom the supposed merit or demerit of original sin or righteous is premised to be imputed ; so that both Adam and each individual of mankind are wholly excluded from acting any part in the premised act of imputation ; and are supposed to be altogether passive in the matter, and consequently it necessarily follows, that if there ever was such an act as that of imputation, it must have been the immediate and sovereign act of God, to the preclusion of the praise or blame of man But to suppose, that God can impute the virtue or vice of the person of A, to be the virtue or vice of the person of B, is the same as to suppose that God can impute or change truth into falsehood, or falsehood into truth, or that he can reverse the nature of moral rectitude itself, which is inadmissable. But admitting, that imputation was in the power and at the option of man, it is altogether probable that they would have been very sparing in imputing merit and happiness, but might nevertheless have been vastly liberal in imputing demerit and misery, from one to another, which is too farcical.

SECTION III.

CONTAINING REMARKS ON THE ATONEMENT AND SATISFACTION FOR ORIGINAL SIN.

The doctrine of imputation is in every point of view incompatible with the moral perfections of God. We will premise, that the race of Adom in their respective generations was guilty of the apostacy, and obnoxious to the vindictive justice and punishment of God, and accordingly doomed to either an eternal or temporary punishment therefore, which is the Bible representation of the matter. What possibility could there have been of reversing the divine decree? It must be supposed to have been just, or it could not have had the divine sanction, and if so, a reversal of it would be unjust. But it would be still a greater injustice to lay the blame and vindictive punishment of a guilty race of condemned sinners upon an innocent and inoffensive being, for in this case the guilty would be exempted from their just punishment, and the innocent unjustly suffer for it, which

7

holds up to view two manifest injustices; the first consists in not doing justice to the guilty, and the second in actually punishing the innocent, which instead of atoning for sin, would add sin to sin, or injustice to injustice; and after all, if it was ever just, that the race of Adam should have been punished for the imputed sin of their premised original ancestor, be that punishment what it will, it is so still, notwithstanding the atonement, for the eternal justice and reason of things can never be altered. This justice always defeats the possibility of satisfaction for sin by way of a mediator.

That physical evils may and have been propagated by natural generation, none can dispute, for that the facts themselves are obvious. But that moral evil can be thus propagated, is altogether chimerical, for we are not born criminals.

SECTION IV.

REMARKS ON REDEMPTION, WROUGHT OUT BY INFLICTING THE DEMERITS OF SIN UPON THE INNOCENT, WOULD BE UNJUST, AND THAT IT COULD CONTAIN NO MERCY OR GOODNESS TO THE UNIVERSALITY OF BEING.

THE practice of imputing one person's crime to another, in capital offences among men, so that the innocent should suffer for the guilty, has never yet been introduced into any court of judicature in the world, or so much as practised in any civilized country; and the manifest reason in this, as in all other cases of imputation, is the same, viz. it confounds personal merit and demerit.

The murderer ought to suffer for the demerit of his crime, but if the court exclude the idea of personal demerit (guilt being always the inherent property of the guilty and of them only) they might as well sentence one person to death for the murder as another : for justice would be wholly blind was it not predicated on the idea of the fact of a personal demerit, on the identical person who was guilty of the murder : nor is it possible to reward merit abstractly considered from its personal agents. These are facts that universally hold good in human government. The same reasons cannot fail to hold good in the divine mind as in that of the human, for the rules of justice are essentially the same whether applied to the one or to the other, having their uniformity in the eternal truth and reason of things.

But it is frequently objected, that inasmuch as one person can pay, satisfy and discharge a cash debt for another, redeem him from prison and set him at liberty, therefore Jesus Christ might become sponsible for the sins of mankind, or of the elect, and by suffering their punishments atone for them and free them from their condemnation. But it should be considered, that comparisons darken or reflect light upon an argument according as they are either pertinent or impertinent thereto ; we will therefore examine the comparison, and see if it will with propriety apply to the atonement.

Upon the Christian scheme, Christ the Son was God, and equal with God the Father, or with God the Holy Ghost, and therefore original sin must be considered to be an offence equally against each of the persons of the premised Trinity, and being of a criminal nature could not be discharged or satisfied by cash or produce, as debts of a civil contract are, but by suffering ; and it has already been proved to be inconsistent with the divine or human government, to inflict the punishment of the guilty upon the innocent, though one man may discharge another's debt in cases where lands, chattels or cash are adequate to it ; but what capital offender was ever discharged by such commodities ?

Still there remains a difficulty on the part of Christianity, in accounting for one of the persons in the premised Trinity satisfying a debt due to the impartial justice of the unity of the three persons. For God the Son to suffer the condemnation of guilt in behalf of man, would not only be unjust in itself, but incompatible with his divinity, and the retribution of the justice of the premised Trinity of persons in the god-head (of whom God the Son must be admitted to be one) toward mankind; for this would be the same as to suppose God to be judge, criminal and executioner, which is inadmissible.

But should we admit for argument's sake, that God suffered for original sin, yet taking into one complex idea the whole mental system of beings, universally, both finite and infinite, there could have been no display of grace, mercy, or goodness to being in general, in such a supposed redemption of mankind ; inasmuch as the same quantity or degree of evil is supposed to have taken place upon being, universally considered, as would have taken place, had finite individuals, or the race of Adam, suffered according to their respective demerits.

Should we admit that there is a Trinity of persons in

the divine essence, yet the one could not suffer without the other, for essence cannot be divided in suffering, any more than in enjoyment. The essence of God is that which includes the divine nature, and the same identical nature must necessarily partake of the same glory, honor, power, wisdom, goodness and absolute uncreated and unlimited perfection, and is equally exempted from weakness and suffering. Therefore, as certain as Christ suffered he was not God, but whether he is supposed to be God or man, or both, he could not in justice have suffered for original sin, which must have been the demerit of its perpetrators as before argued.

Supposing Christ to have been both God and man, he must have existed in two distinct essences, viz. the essence of God and the essence of man. And if he existed in two distinct and separate essences, there could be no union between the divine and human natures. But if there is any such thing as an hypostatical union between the divine and human natures, it must unite both in one essence, which is impossible : for the divine nature being infinite, could admit of no addition or enlargement and consequently cannot allow of a union with any nature whatever. Was such an union possible in itself, yet, for a superior nature to unite with an inferior one in the same essence, would be degrading to the former, as it would put both natures on a level by constituting an identity of nature : the consequences whereof would either deify man, or divest God of his divinity, and reduce him to the rank and condition of a creature ; inasmuch as the united essence must be denominated either divine or human.

CHAPTER XII.

SECTION I.

OF THE IMPOSSIBILITY OF TRANSLATING AN INFALLIBLE
REVELATION FROM ITS ORIGINAL COPIES, AND PRE-
SERVING IT ENTIRE THROUGH ALL THE REVOLUTIONS
OF THE WORLD, AND VICISSITUDES OF HUMAN LEARN-
ING TO OUR TIME.

ADMITTING for argument sake that the Scriptures of
the Old and New Testament were originally of divine
supernatural inspiration, and that their first manuscript
copies were the infallible institutions of God, yet to trace
them from their respective ancient dead languages, and
different and diverse translations, from the obscure hieroglyphical pictures of characters, in which they were first
written, through all the vicissitudes and alterations of
human learning, prejudices, superstitions, enthusiasms
and diversities of interests and manners, to our time, so
as to present us with a perfect edition from its premised
infallible original manuscript copies would be impossible.
The various and progressive methods of learning, with
the insurmountable difficulties of translating any supposed antiquated written revelation would not admit of
it, as the succeeding observations on language and grammar will fully evince.

In those early ages of learning, hieroglyphics were
expressive of ideas ; for instance, a snake quirled (a position common to that venomous reptile) was an emblem
of eternity, and the picture of a lion, a representation of
power, and so every beast, bird, reptile, insect and fish,

had in their respective pictures, particular ideas annexed to them, which varied with the arbitrary custom and common consent of the several separate nations, among whom this way of cummunicating ideas was practised, in some sense analogous to what is practised at this day by different nations, in connecting particular ideas to certain sounds or words written in characters, which according to certain rules of grammar constitute the several languages. But the hieroglyphical manner of writing by living emblems, and perhaps in some instances by other pictures, was very abstruse, and inadequate to communicate that multiplicity and diversity of ideas which are requisite for the purpose of history, argumentation or general knowledge in any of the sciences or concerns of life; which mystical way of communicating ideas underwent a variety of alterations and improvements, though not so much as that of characters and grammar has done; for in the hieroglyphical way of communicating their ideas, there was no such thing as spelling, or what is now called orthography, which has been perpetually refining and altering, ever since characters, syllables, words or grammar have been brought into use, and which will admit of correction and improvement as long as mankind continue in the world. For which reason the original of all languages is absorbed and lost in the multiplicity of alterations and refinements, which have in all ages taken place, so that it is out of the power of all Etymologists and Lexiconists now living, to explain the ideas, which were anciently connected with those hieroglyphical figures or words, and which may have composed the original of any language, written in characters,

in those obsolete and antiquated ages, when learning and
science were in their infancy : since the beneficial art of
printing has arrived to any considerable degree of perfection, the etymology of words, in the scientifical and
learned languages, has been considerably well understood : though imperfectly, as the various opinions of the
learned concerning it may witness.   But since the
era of printing, the knowledge of the ancient learning
has been in a great measure, or in most respects, wholly
lost ; and inasmuch as the modern substitute is much
better, it is no loss at all.   Some of the old English authors are at this day quite unintelligible, and others in
their respective latter publications, more or less so.   The
last century and a half has done more towards the perfecting of grammar, and purifying the languages than
the world had ever done before.

   I do not understand Latin, Greek or Hebrew, in which
languages, it is said, that the several original manuscripts
of the Scriptures were written ; but I am informed by
the learned therein, that, like other languages, they have
gone through their respective alterations and refinements,
which must have been the case, except they reached their
greatest perfection in their first composition ; of which
the progressive condition of man could not admit.   So
that the learned in those languages, at this day, know
but little or nothing how they were spoken or written
when the first manuscript copies of the Scriptures were
composed ; and consequently, are not able to inform us,
whether their present translations do, any of them, perfectly agree with their respective original premised infallible manuscript copies or not.   And inasmuch as the

several English translations of the Bible do materially differ from each other, it evinces the confused and blundering condition in which it has been handed down to us.

The clergy often informs us from the desk, that the translation of the Bible, which is now in use in this country, is erroneous, after having read such and such a passage of it, in either Latin, Greek or Hebrew, they frequently give us to understand, that instead of the present translation, it should have been rendered thus and thus in English, but never represent to us how it was read and understood in the antiquated and mystical figures or characters of those languages, when the manuscripts of Scripture were first written, or how it has been preserved and handed down entire, through every refinement of those languages, to the present condition of Latin, Greek and Hebrew. Probably this is too abstruse a series of retrospective learning for their scholarship, and near or quite as foreign from their knowledge as from that of their hearers.

It is not to be supposed that all the alterations which have taken place in language, have been merely by improving it. In many instances, ignorance, accident or custom has varied it to its disadvantage, but it has nevertheless been subject to correction, and generally speaking has been altered for the better, yet, by one means or other has been so fluctuating and unstable, as that an infallible revelation could not have been genuinely preserved, through all the vicissitudes and revolutions of learning, for more than seventeen hundred years last past to this day.

7 *

The diversity of the English language is represented
with great accuracy by Mr. Samuel Johnson, the celebrated lexicographer, in the samples of different ages, in
his history of the English language, subjoined to the
preface of the dictionary, to which the curious are referred for the observance of the various specimens.

———— •

SECTION II.

THE VARIETY OF ANNOTATIONS AND EXPOSITIONS OF THE SCRIRTURES, TOGETHER WITH THE DIVERSITY OF SECTARIES EVINCES THEIR FALLIBILITY.

EVERY commentary and annotation on the Bible, implicitly declares its fallibility; for if the Scriptures remained genuine and entire, they would not stand in need
of commentaries and expositions, but would shine in
their infallible lustre and purity without them. What
an idle phantom it is for mortals to assay to illustrate and
explain to mankind, that which God may be supposed to
have undertaken to do, by the immediate inspiration of
his spirit? Do they understand how to define or explain
it better than God may be supposed to have done? This
is not supposable; upon what ground then do these
multiplicity of comments arise, except it be pre-supposed
that the present translations of the Bible have, by some
means or other, become fallible and imperfect, and therefore need to be rectified and explained? and if so, it has
lost the stamp of divine authority; provided in its original composition it may be supposed to have been possessed of it.

To construe or spiritualize the Bible is the same as to inspire it over again, by the judgment, fancy or enthusiasm of men; and thus the common people, by receiving God's supposed revelation at secondary hands (whether at the thousandth or ten thousandth remove from its first premised inspiration they know not) cannot in fact be taught by the revelation of God. Add to this the diverse and clashing expositions of the Bible, among which are so many flagrant proofs of the fallibility and uncertainty of such teachings, as must convince even bigots, that every one of these expositions are erroneous, *except their own!*

It has been owing to different comments on the Scriptures, that Christians have been divided into sectaries. Every commentator, who could influence a party to embrace his comment, put himself, at the head of a division of Christians; as Luther, Calvin, and Arminius, laid the foundation of the sectaries who bear their names; and the Socinians were called after the Scismatical Socinius; the same may be said of each of the sectaries. Thus it is that different commentaries or acceptations of the original meaning of the Scriptures, have divided the Christian world into divisions and subdivisions of which it consists at present. Nor was there ever a division or subdivision among Jews, Christians or Mahometans, respecting their notions or opinions of religion, but what was occasioned by commentating on the Scriptures, or else by latter pretended inspired revelations from God in addition thereto. The law of Moses was the first pretended immediate revelation from God, which respects the Bible, and after that in succession the several revelations of the prophets, and last of all (in the Chsistian system) the revelations of Jesus Christ and apostles, who challenged a right of abolishing the priesthood of Moses; Christ claiming to be the antitype of which the institution of sacrifices and ceremonial part of the law of Moses was emblematical; but this infringement of the prerogative of the Levitical priests gave such offence, not only to them, but to the Jews as a nation, that they rejected Christianity, and have not subscribed to the divine authority of it to this day, holding to the law of Moses and the prophets. However Christianity made a great progress in the world, and has been very much divided into sectaries, by the causes previously assigned.

"Mahomet taking notice of the numerous sects and divisions among Christians, in his journies to Palestine, &c., thought it would not be difficult to introduce a new religion, and make himself high priest and sovereign of the people." This he finally effected, prosecuting his scheme so far, that he new modelled the Scriptures, presenting them, (as he said,) in their original purity, and called his disciples after his own name. He gained great numbers of proselytes and became their sovereign in civil, military and spiritual matters, instituted the order of mystical priesthood, and gave the world a new Bible by the name of the Alcoran; which he gives us to understand was communicated to him from God, by the intermediate agency of the angel Gabriel, chapter by chapter. "His disciples at this day inhabit a great part of the richest countries in the world, and are supposed to be more numerous than the Christians," and are as much, if not more, divided into sectaries, from causes similar to those which produced the division of Christians, viz.: the different commentators on, and exposi-

tions of the Alcoran. The Mufti, or priests, represented the doctrines and precepts of the Alcoran in a
variety of lights different from each other, each of them
claiming the purity of the original and infallible truths
prescribed to the world by Mahomet, their great reformer
of Christianity. For though the several sectaries of
Mahometans differ, respecting the meaning of their Alcoran, yet they all hold to the truth and divine authority
thereof, the same as the Christian sectaries do concerning their Bible: so that all the different opinions which
ever did, or at present do subsist, between Jews, Christians and Mahometans, may be resolved into one consideration, viz.: the want of a right understanding of the
original of the Scriptures. All sat out at first, as they
imagined, from the truth of God's word, (except the
impostors,) concluded that they had an infallible guide,
and have, by one means or other, been guided into as
many opposite faiths as human invention has been capable of fabricating; each sect among the whole, exulting
in their happy ignorance, believing that they are favored
with an infallible revelation for their direction.

It alters not the present argument, whether the Scriptures were originally true or not; for though they be
supposed to have been either true or false, or a mixture
of both, yet they could never have been handed down
entire and uncorrupted to the present time, through the
various changes and perpetual refinements of learning
and language; this is not merely a matter of speculative
and argumentative demonstration, the palpable certainty
of it stands confessed in every Jewish, Christian and
Mahometan sectary.

SECTION III.

ON THE COMPILING OF THE MANUSCRIPTS OF THE SCRIP-
TURES INTO ONE VOLUME, AND OF ITS SEVERAL TRANS-
LATIONS.　THE INFALLIBILITY OF THE POPES, AND OF
THEIR CHARTERED RIGHTS TO REMIT OR RETAIN SINS,
AND OF THE IMPROPRIETY OF THEIR BEING TRUSTED
WITH A REVELATION FROM GOD.

THE manuscripts of Scripture, which are said to have
been originally written on scrolls of bark, long before
the invention of paper or printing, and are said to
compose our present Bible, were in a loose and confused condition, scattered about in the world, deposited
nobody knows how or where, and at different times were
compiled into one volume.　The four gospels are by
the learned generally admitted to have been wrote many
years after Christ, particularly that of St. John: and
sundry other gospels in the primitive ages of Christianity
were received as divine by some of its then sectaries,
which have unfortunately not met with approbation in
subsequent eras of the despotism of the church.

The translation of the Scriptures by Ptolemy Phila-
delphus, king of Egypt, was before Christ, and therefore could not include the writings of the New Testament in his translation, and " whether by seventy-two
interpreters, and in the manner as is commonly related,
is justly questioned."　But where, at what time, and by
whom, the Scriptures of the Old and New Testament
were first compiled into one volume, is what I do not
understand: but was it a longer or shorter period after
Christ, it alters not the present argument materially,

since the scattered manuscripts were in a loose and confused condition for a long time; and the grand query is, when the compilers of those manuscripts collected them together in order to form them into one volume, how they could have understood the supposed divine writings, or symbolical figures, with the ideas originally connected with them, and distinguish them from those which were merely human, and in comparison of the others are called profane. To understand this distinction would require a new revelation, as much as may be supposed necessary for composing the original manuscripts themselves; but it is not pretended that the compilers or translators of the Bible were inspired by the divine spirit in the doing and completing their respective business; so that human reason, fancy, or some latent design, must needs have been substituted, in distinguishing the supposed divine and human writings apart, and in giving a perfect transcript of the original manuscripts. Now admitting that the compilers were really honest principled men, (which is more than we are certain of,) it would follow, that they would be obliged to cull out of the mixed mass of premised divine and human writings, such as to them appeared to be divine, which would make them to be the sole arbitrators of the divinity that they were compiling to be handed down to posterity as the infallible word of God, which is a great stretch of prerogative for mortal and fallible man to undertake, and as great a weakness in others to subscribe to it, as of divine authority.

Mr. Fenning, in his dictionary definition of the word Bible, subjoins the following history of its translations:

"The translation of this sacred volume was begun very early in this kingdom," [England,] "and some part of it was done by King Alfred. Adelmus translated the Psalms into Saxon in 709, other parts were done by Edfrid or Ecbert in 730, the whole by Bede in 731. Trevisa published the whole in English in 1357. Tindals was brought higher in 1534, revised and altered in 1538, published with a preface of Cranmers in 1540. In 1551, another translation was published, which was revised by several bishops, was printed with their altera- tions in 1560. In 1607, a new translation was published by authority, which is that in present use." From this account it appears, that from the first translation of the Bible by Trevisa, into English, in 1357, it has been revised, altered, and passed through six different pub- lications, the last of which is said to have been done by authority, which I conclude means that of the king, whose prerogative in giving us a divine revelation, can no more be esteemed valid than that of other men, though he may be possessed of an arbitrary power within the limits of his realm to prevent any further correction and publication of it. As to the changes it underwent previous to Trevisa's translation, in which time it was most exposed to corruptions of every kind, we will not at present particularly consider, but only observe that those translations could not, every one of them, be per- fect, since they were diverse from each other, in conse- quence of their respective revisions and corrections; nor is it possible that the Bible, in any of its various edi- tions could be perfect, any more than all and every one of those persons who have acted a part in transmitting them down to our time may be supposed to be so : for perfection does not pertain to man, but is the essential prerogative of God.

The Roman Catholics, to avoid the evils of imperfection, fallibility and imposture of man, have set up the Pope to be infallible; this is their security against being misguided in their faith, and by ascribing holiness to him, secure themselves from imposture ; a deception which is incompatible with holiness. So that in matters of faith, they have nothing more to do, but to believe as their church believes. Their authority for absolving or retaining sins is very extraordinary ; however, their charter is from Christ, (admitting them to be his vicars, and the successors of St. Peter,) and the present English translation of the Bible warrants it. The commission is in these words : "And I will give unto thee the keys of the kingdom of heaven, and whoever thou shalt bind on earth, shall be bound in heaven ; and whatsoever thou shall loose on earth, shall be loosed in heaven. Whosoever sins ye remit, they are remitted unto them, and whosoever sins ye retain, they are retained." That St. Peter or his successors should have a power of binding and determining the state and condition of mankind in the world to come by remitting or retaining sins, is too great a power to be intrusted to men, as it interferes with the providence and prerogative of God, who on this position would be exempted from judging the world, (as it would interfere with the chartered prerogative of the Popes in their remitting or retaining of sins, admitting it to have been genuine,) precluding the divine retribution of justice ; we may, therefore, from the authority of reason, conclude it to be spurious. It was a long succession of ages that all christendom were dupes to the See of Rome, in which time it is too evident to be denied, that the holy fathers obtruded a great deal of pious fraud on their devotees; all public worship was read to the people in unknown languages, as it is to this day in Roman Catholic countries. Nor has the Bible, in those countries, to this time, been permitted to be published in any but the learned languages, which affords great opportunity to the Romish church to fix it to answer their lucrative purposes. Nor is it to be supposed that they want the inclination to do it. The before recited grant of the power of the absolution of sin, to St Peter in particular, was undoubtedly of their contrivance.

In short, reason would prompt us to conclude, that had God, in very deed, made a revelation of his mind and will to mankind, as a rule of duty and practice to them, and to be continued as such to the latest posterity, he would in the course of his providence have ordered matters so that it should have been deposited, translated, and kept, in the hands of men of a more unexceptionable character than those holy cheats can pretend to.

Witchcraft and priestcraft, were introduced into this world together, in its non-age; and has gone on, hand in hand together, until about half a century past, when witchcraft began to be discredited, and is at present almost exploded, both in Europe and America. This discovery has depreciated priestcraft, on the scale of at least fifty per cent. per annum, and rendered it highly probable that the improvement of succeeding generations, in the knowledge of nature and science, will exalt the reason of mankind, above the tricks and impostures of priests, and bring them back to the religion of nature and truth; ennoble their minds, and be the means of cultivating concord, and mutual love in society, and of extending charity, and good will to all intelligent beings throughout the universe; exalt the divine character, and lay a permanent foundation for truth and reliance on providence; establish our hopes and prospects of immortality, and be condusive to every desirable consequence, in this world, and that which is to come; which will crown the scene of human felicity in this sublunary state of being and probation; which can never be completed while we are under the power and tyranny of priests, since as it ever has, it ever will be their interest, to invalidate the law of nature and reason, in order to establish systems incompatible therewith.

CHAPTER XIII.

SECTION I.

MORALITY DERIVED FROM NATURAL FITNESS, AND NOT FROM TRADITION.

Such parts or passages of the Scriptures as inculcate morality, have a tendency to subserve mankind, the same as all other public investigations or teachings of it, may be supposed to have; but are neither better or worse for having a place in the volume of those writings denominated canonical; for morality does not derive its nature from books, but from the fitness of things; and though it may be more or less, interspersed through the pages of the Alcoran, its purity and rectitude would remain the same; for it is founded in eternal right; and whatever writings, books or oral speculations, best illustrate or teach this moral science, should have the preference. The knowledge of this as well as all other sciences, is acquired from reason and experience, and (as it is progressively obtained) may with propriety be called, the revelation of God, which he has revealed to us in the constitution of our rational natures; and as it is congenial with reason and truth, cannot (like other revelations) partake of imposture. This is natural religion, and could be derived from none other but God. I have endeavored, in this treatise, to prune this religion from those excrescences, with which craft on the one hand, and ignorance on the other, have loaded it; and to hold it up to view in its native simplicity, free from alloy; and have throughout the contents of the volume, addressed the reason of mankind, and not their passions, traditions or prejudices; for which cause, it is noways probable that it will meet with any considerable approbation.

Most of the human race, by one means or other are prepossessed with principles opposed to the religion of reason. In these parts of America, they are most generally taught, that they are born into the world in a state of enmity to God and moral good, and are under his wrath and curse, that the way to heaven and future blessedness is out of their power to pursue, and that it is incumbered with mysteries which none but the priests can unfold, that we must "*be born again,*" have a special kind of faith, and be regenerated; or in fine, that human nature, which they call " the old man," must be destroyed, perverted, or changed by them, and by them new modelled, before it can be admitted into the heavenly kingdom. Such a plan of superstition, as far as it obtains credit in the world, subjects mankind to sacerdotal empire; which is erected on the imbecility of human nature. Such of mankind, as break the fetters of their education, remove such other obstacles as are in their way, and have the confidence publicly to talk rational, exalt reason to its just supremacy, and vindicate truth and the ways of God's providence to men, are sure to be stamped with the epithet of irreligious, infidel, profane, and the like. But it is often observed of such a man, that he is *morally honest,* and as often replied, *what of that? Morality will carry no man to heaven.* So that all the satisfaction the honest man can have while the superstitious are squibbling hell fire at him, is to retort back upon them that they are priest ridden.

The manner of the existence, and intercourse of human souls, after the dissolution of their bodies by death, being inconceiveable to us in this life, and all manner of intelligence between us and departed souls impracticable, the priests have it in their power to amuse us with a great variety of visionary apprehensions of things in the world to come, which, while in this life, we cannot contradict from experience, the test of great part of our certainty (especially to those of ordinary understandings) and having introduced mysteries into their religion, make it as incomprehensible to us, (in this natural state) as the

manner of our future existence ; and from Scripture authority, having invalidated reason as being carnal and depraved, they proceed further to teach us from the same
authority, that, "the natural man knoweth not the things
of the spirit, for they are foolishness unto him, neither
can he know them for they are spiritually discerned."
A spiritualizing teacher is nearly as well acquainted with
the kingdom of heaven, as a man can be with his home
lot.   He knows the road to heaven and eternal blessedness, to which happy regions, with the greatest assurance,
he presumes to pilot his dear disciples and unfold to them
the mysteries of the canonical writings, and of the world
to come; they catch the enthusiasm and see with the
same sort of spiritual eyes, with which they can pierce
religion through and through, and understand the spiritual meaning of the Scriptures, which before had been "a
dead letter" to them, particularly the revelations of St.
John the divine, and the allusion of the horns therein
mentioned.   The most obscure and unintelligible passages
of the Bible, come within the compass of their spiritual
discerning as apparently as figures do to a mathmetician :
then they can sing songs out of the Canticles, saying, " I
am my beloved's and my beloved is mine ; " and being
at a loose from the government of reason, please themselves with any fanaticisms they like best, as that of their
being "snatched as brands out of the burning, to enjoy
the special and eternal favor of God, not from any worthi-
ness or merit in them, but merely from the sovereign will
and pleasure of God, while millions of millions, as good
by nature and practice as they, were left to welter eternally, under the scalding drops of divine vengeance ; "

not considering, that if it was consistent with the perfections of God to save them, his salvation could not fail to have been uniformly extended to all others, whose circumstances may be supposed to be similar to, or more deserving than theirs, for equal justice cannot fail to apply in all cases in which equal justice demands it. But these deluded people resolve the divine government altogether into sovereignty : " even so Father, for so it seemed good in thy sight." And as they exclude reason and justice from their imaginary notions of religion, they also exclude it from the providence or moral government of God. Nothing is more common, in the part of the country where I was educated, than to hear those infatuated people, in their public and private addresses, acknowledge to their creator, from the desk and elsewhere, " hadst thou, O Lord, laid judgment to the line and righteousness to the plummet, we had been in the grave with the dead and in hell with the damned, long before this time." Such expressions from the creature to the creator are profane, and utterly incompatible with the divine character. Undoubtedly, (all things complexly considered) the providence of God to man is just, inasmuch as it has the divine approbation.

The superstitious thus set up a spiritual discerning, independent of, and in opposition to reason, and their mere imaginations pass with each other, and with themselves, for infallible truth. Hence it is, that they despise the progressive and wearisome reasonings of philosophers (which must be admitted to be a painful method of arriving at truth) but as it is the only way in which we can acquire it, I have pursued the old natural road of racioc-

a q

ination, concluding, that as this spiritual discerning is altogether inadequate to the management of any of the concerns of life, or of contributing any assistance or knowledge towards the perfecting of the arts and sciences, it is equally unintelligible and insignificant in matters of religion : and therefore conclude, that if the human race in general, could be prevailed upon to exercise common sense in religious concerns, those spiritual fictions would cease, and be succeeded by reason and truth.

SECTION II.

OF THE IMPORTANCE OF THE EXERCISE OF REASON, AND PRACTICE OF MORALITY, IN ORDER TO THE HAPPINESS OF MANKIND.

THE period of life is very uncertain, and at the longest is but short; a few years bring us from infancy to man-hood, a few more to a dissolution ; pain, sickness and death are the necessary consequences of animal life. Through life we struggle with physical evils, which eventually are certain to destroy our earthly composition ; and well would it be for us did evils end here ; but alas ! moral evil has been more or less predominant in our agency, and though natural evil is unavoidable, yet moral evil may be prevented or remedied by the exercise of virtue. Morality is therefore of more importance to us than any or all other attainments ; as it is a habit of mind, which, from a retrospective consciousness of our agency in this life, we should carry with us into our succeeding

state of existence, as an acquired appendage of our
rational nature, and as the necessary means of our mental
happiness. Virtue and vice are the only things in this
world, which, with our souls, are capable of surviving
death; the former is the rational and only procuring
cause of all intellectual happiness, and the latter of conscious guilt and misery; and therefore, our indispensable
duty and ultimate interest is, to love, cultivate and
improve the one, as the means of our greatest good, and
to hate and abstain from the other, as productive of our
greatest evil. And in order thereto, we should so far
divest ourselves of the incumbrances of this world, (which
are too apt to engross our attention) as to inquire a consistent system of the knowledge of religious duty, and
make it our constant endeavor in life to act conformably
to it. The knowledge of the being, perfections, creation
and providence of God, and of the immortality of our
souls, is the foundation of religion; which has been
particularly illustrated in the four first chapters of this
discourse. And as the Pagan, Jewish, Christian and
Mahometan countries of the world have been overwhelm-
ed with a multiplicity of revelations diverse from each
other, and which, by their respective promulgators, are
said to have been immediately inspired into their souls
by the spirit of God, or immediately communicated to
them by the intervening agency of angels (as in the
instance of the invisible Gabriel to Mahomet) and as those
revelations have been received and credited, by afar the
greater part of the inhabitants of the several countries of
the world (on whom they have been obtruded) as supernaturally revealed by God or angels, and which, in

8

doctrine and discipline, are in most respects repugnant to each other, it fully evinces their imposture, and authorizes us, without a lengthy course of arguing, to determine with certainty, that not one of them had their original from God ; as they clash with each other, which is ground of high probability against the authenticity of each of them.

A revelation, that may be supposed to be really of the institution of God, must also be supposed to be perfectly consistent or uniform, and to be able to stand the test of truth ; therefore such pretended revelations, as are tendered to us as the contrivance of heaven, which do not bear that test, we may be morally certain, was either originally a deception, or has since, by adulteration become spurious.

Reason therefore must be the standard by which we determine the respective claims of revelation ; for otherwise we may as well subscribe to the divinity of the one as of the other, or to the whole of them, or to none at all. So likewise on this thesis, if reason rejects the whole of those revelations, we ought to return to the religion of nature and reason.

Undoubtedly it is our duty, and for our best good, that we occupy and improve the faculties, with which our creator has endowed us, but so far as prejudice, or prepossession of opinion prevails over our minds, in the same proportion, reason is excluded from our theory or practice. Therefore if we would acquire useful knowledge, we must first divest ourselves of those impediments ; and sincerely endeavor to search out the truth : and draw our conclusions from reason and just argument, which will never conform to our inclination, interest or fancy ; but we must conform to that if we would judge rightly. As certain as we determine contrary to reason, we make a wrong conclusion ; therefore, our wisdom is, to conform to the nature and reason of things, as well in religious matters, as in other sciences. Preposterously absurd would it be, to negative the exercise of reason in religious concerns, and yet, be actuated by it in all other and less occurrences of life. All our knowledge of things is derived from God, in and by the order of nature, out of which we cannot perceive, reflect or understand any thing whatsoever ; our external senses are natural ; and those objects are also natural ; so that ourselves, and all things about us, and our knowledge collected therefrom, is natural, and not supernatural ; as argued in the fifth chapter.

An unjust composition never fails to contain error and falsehood. Therefore an unjust connection of ideas is not derived from nature, but from the imperfect composition of man. Misconnection of ideas is the same as misjudging, and has no positive existence, being merely a creature of the imagination ; but nature and truth are real and uniform ; and the rational mind by reasoning, discerns the uniformity, and is thereby enabled to make a just composition of ideas, which will stand the test of truth. But the fantastical illuminations of the credulous and superstitious part of mankind, proceed from weakness, and as far as they take place in the world subvert the religion of REASON, NATURE and TRUTH.

ETHAN ALLEN.